THE EUCHARISTIC YEAR

Seasonal Devotions for the Sacrament

A. H. BAVERSTOCK

with an introduction by

JULIAN LITTEN

MOREHOUSE PUBLISHING

Morehouse Publishing is a division of The Morehouse Group.

Text © A. H. Baverstock 1930
Introduction © Julien Litten 2001

First published in Great Britain as *Annus Eucharisticus*
by the Faith Press in 1930
This edition published in Great Britain in 2001
by Canterbury Press Norwich
St Mary's Works, St Mary's Plain,
Norwich, Norfolk NR3 3BH
First North American edition published in the
United States of America in 2002
by Morehouse Publishing

A Catalog record for this book is available from the
Library of Congress.
ISBN 1–8192–1900–2

Printed in Great Britain
02 03 04 05 06 5 4 3 2 1

FOREWORD

By the Viscount Halifax.

Alleluya! Not as orphans
Are we left in sorrow now;
Alleluya! He is with us,
Faith believes, nor questions how;
Though the cloud from sight received him
When the forty days were o'er,
Shall our hearts forget his promise,
I am with you evermore?

But is not that precisely what so many of us do? Can we pretend that, for the most part, we adequately realise in what the Christian life consists, what is its glory, the source of its joy, and of its abiding strength? Is it not, to use St. Paul's own words, the being "in Christ"? "Christ in us, the hope of glory," expresses the fact which it most concerns us to realise. What words can be more explicit than those of our Lord himself in stating this fact?

On the morning of his Resurrection he promises St. Mary Magdalen, who had striven to touch his feet, that after his Ascension the presence she had sought should be hers. On the same day at even, after assuring his Disciples that it was he himself in the reality of his human body and no spirit, who had come to them, he goes on to say, "He will not leave them comfortless, but will come to them. The world will not see him, but they will see him, and his joy will be fulfilled in themselves." The doubt expressed by St. Thomas is referred to in order to express the blessedness of those who, " not having seen, yet have believed " in his presence in regard to which he promises that he will be present with them till the end of the world.

In what respect, then, does his presence, so promised and abiding with us now, differ from his presence vouchsafed to the world during the forty days after his Resurrection; except that in the one case he was visible to all, and in the other, only visible when it so pleased him.

So to realise his presence is to be armed against the world, the flesh and the devil. It is the secret of the consistent Christian life; and the ignorance of Christian belief and practice which so largely prevails amongst us, and is so great a distress to all who care for the welfare of the Christian religion and the honour and glory of our Lord Jesus Christ, is the result of ignoring so vital a part of what is essential Church teaching.

The extracts from the writings of the Fathers and the meditations those extracts suggest, arranged for every day of the year, are another effort to bring home to the minds of all what the most blessed Sacrament means to Christian people, from one whose whole life has been spent in unwearied work for the glory of God and the good of souls, in the Anglican Communion.

PREFACE.

BY THE COMPILER.

OUR times have seen a great revival in the English Church of devotion to the Blessed Sacrament of the Altar. The object of this compilation is to serve such devotion. The Church of England at the Reformation appealed to the teaching of the early Fathers. Here will be found abundant evidence of the fervour of their faith and devotion in regard to the Mass and the Blessed Sacrament. There has been of late frequent insistence on the fact that many of the forms which modern devotion to the Blessed Sacrament has taken are mediæval or modern rather than primitive. It seems of some importance to show that the basis of devotion, the conviction that the Blessed Sacrament is our Lord himself, present as Victim and Food, and the Object of divine worship, is as clear in the faith of the primitive Church as in our own. Not only that, but the forms by which such devotion was expressed were of like nature to the modern forms. We do not, it is true, find in the primitive Mass the elevation immediately after consecration, with the ringing of a sanctus bell; we do not find Exposition and Benediction in the form in which they prevail in Western Christendom to-day. But we do find an exposition of the Blessed Sacrament with accompanying prostrations on the part of the worshippers, immediately before Communion. Primitive writers, St. Chrysostom in particular, lay emphasis on the looking upon the divine Victim seen by the eye of faith while the bodily gaze is fixed upon the uplifted Host and Cup. And we find the faithful blessing themselves with the holy Sacrament as they take it from the priest, kissing it and putting it to their eyes, with the approval of their teachers. We are in the same world of ideas : there is the same loving devotion to him, who, having given himself for us on Calvary, gives no less than himself to us at the Altar.

A. H. BAVERSTOCK.

INTRODUCTION

The Society of the Faith and Faith Press

The Society of the Faith came into being in August 1905 at a meeting in the church of St Andrew, Portland Place, London. It began at the instigation of two notable figures of the Catholic Revival, the Revd Canon Dr John Albert Douglas, vicar of Luke's, Camberwell and his brother, the Revd Charles Edward Douglas who, with a group of like-minded friends, formed what they later described as

> 'an Association of Christians in communion with the See of Canterbury for mutual assistance in the work of Christ's Church and for the furtherance of such charitable undertakings as may be from time to time decided upon, more especially for the popularisation of the Catholic Faith.'

The Society lost no time in putting these principles into practice. Their first publication venture was the 'stamp system' for Sunday Schools, directed towards those whom it called 'The Children of the Childermote'. From this humble beginning developed the weightier Faith Press Limited, established in 1913, with its own type-setting and printing press facilities at Leighton Buzzard and a sales outlet at 22 Buckingham Street, Charing Cross. Its first publication was *The Young Christian's Progress* by Canon J A Douglas followed in 1914 by its sequel, *The Home of Mother Church*, a guide to the ornaments of the Church, again by Canon J A Douglas and with illustrations by T Noyes Lewis. For the next sixty years Faith Press developed into a major publisher of Church literature and music, including the responsibility for publishing the Archbishop of Canterbury's Lent book, while not abandoning its missionary work amongst children through its various publications in the *Childermote Library* series.

Annus Eucharisticus

In June 1930 Faith Press Limited published *Annus Eucharisticus*, a patristic anthology compiled by the Revd Alban H Baverstock, rector of Hinton Martel, Dorset, with eight tipped-in colour illustrations by T Noyes Lewis of various stages of the Mass[1]. Dedicated to 'all devout communicants of the English Church', Fr Baverstock's anthology was aimed at the laity. The preamble of his Preface explained the reason for the book: 'Our times have seen a great revival in the English Church of devotion to the Blessed Sacrament of the Altar. The object of this compilation is to serve such devotion . . . Primitive writers, St Chrysostom in particular, lay emphasis on the looking upon the divine Victim by the eye of faith while the bodily gaze is fixed upon the uplifted Host and Cup. And we find the faithful blessing themselves with the holy Sacrament as they take it from the priest, kissing it and putting it to their eyes, with the approval of their teachers.'

Fr Baverstock provided no direction in his Preface as to the reader's use of the book. This duty was left to Lord Halifax, whose Foreword included a tribute to its author: 'The extracts from the writings of the Fathers

---

[1] These were: *The Preparation, The Holy Gospel, The Offertory, Sursum Corda, The Holy Sacrifice, Agnus Dei, The House of Bread* (frontispiece) and *The Blessing*. These illustrations were subsequently issued as postcards by Faith Press.

and the meditations those extracts suggest, arranged for every day of the year, are another effort to bring home to the minds of all what the most blessed Sacrament means to Christian people, from one whose whole life has been spent in wearied work for the glory of God and the good of souls, in the Anglican Communion.' So there we have it: the selected passages were to be used devotionally as meditations on the Sacrament at the daily Mass.

Annus Eucharisticus was not Baverstock's first publishing venture with Faith Press for it had already published *The Unscathed Crucifix* in 1916. Baverstock's highly successful *Priesthood in Liturgy and Life* was first published by Faith Press in 1917 and went into a second edition shortly afterwards. His last sortie with them came in 1933 with *The Compassion of St Mary*, a devotional text based on Our Lady's spiritual involvement in Our Lord's Passion.

How Annus Eucharisticus *was to be used*

The book was arranged to complement the Church's Year according to the Calendar of the *English Missal*, beginning at Advent I and ending at Trinity XXVI, though omitting the major Saint's Days and the lesser feasts. Each week has seven commentaries, being one for each day of the week, with each new week beginning on the Sunday. Precisely how the reader was meant to use the book was left open for interpretation. The commentary could be included in one's preparation prayers before Mass, or used as a personal Communion Antiphon, or as a form of thanksgiving in that period of silence after receiving the Blessed Sacrament.

The work itself was the result of many years reading by Fr Baverstock of patristic writings, noting as he went along those passages relating to the strength and value of the Eucharist. Some eighty authors from the third to the eighth century are referred to, in addition to comments on the Mass from the Council of Arles and the Council of Nicæa, though almost half of his sources are from the writings of St John Chrysostom, St Augustine, St Ambrose, St Cyril of Alexandria and St Ephraem. A full list of the references can be found in the Index.

The Rev'd Fr Alban Baverstock SSC[2]

Alban Henry Baverstock was born on 3rd July 1871 and was baptised by Fr Alexander Maconochie in St Alban's, Holborn twenty-two days later on the Feast of St James. Growing up in the parish of St James, Hatcham, the young Baverstock would have been known to the redoubtable Fr Tooth of St James'. However, the family moved back into Bloomsbury when the child was five, worshipping at St Alban's, Holborn, where they were stalwart members of the congregation. Growing up in the presence of such luminaries as Fr Stanton, Fr Hogg and Fr Suckling it came as little surprise to Baverstock's parents that he wished to seek ordination. After Keble, Oxford, Baverstock had a short period as a teacher in order to raise sufficient capital to get himself through Cuddesden. Ordained priest in December 1896, he served his title at Evesham under Fr George Napier-Whittingham, and then a two-year curacy between 1897–99 at St Michael and All Angels, Walthamstow before receiving his first (and only) living, that of Hinton Martel, Dorset. During his thirty-one years at St John the Evangelist, Hinton

---

[2] The best biography of Baverstock is Revd R J Farmer, *Alban Henry Baverstock 1871–1950*, London (Catholic League) 1997.

Martel[3], Baverstock maintained the daily Mass and, over the years, made it a place of 'uncompromising Anglo-Catholicism'[4]. By 1905 there was a Ward of the Confraternity of the Blessed Sacrament, a statue of Our Lady of Lourdes was set up in 1911 and Stations of the Cross between 1914–18. Processions around the village on Corpus Christi, the Assumption and St Joseph's Day soon became regular annual events.

But it was as a confessor that Fr Baverstock was better known, his confessional being used by clergy and laity throughout the diocese who desired to have the benefit of his counsel and wise advice. Indeed, the experience he himself gained through this ministry resulted in the publication of his book *The Priest as Confessor* in 1914.

In 1903 Baverstock established a children's home in Hinton Martel. Known as St Joseph's it catered for orphans, the mentally handicapped and those from difficult backgrounds, the majority being drawn from the London slums. In 1909 Baverstock took on the role as Warden of the Society of the Holy Crown of Our Lord, a London-based foundation also dedicated to the welfare of mentally handicapped children, and subsequently assisted one of his penitents to establish the Sisters of the Transfiguration at near-by West Moors, Dorset, for the care of mentally retarded girls. Baverstock remained its Visitor until his resignation of the Hinton Martel living in 1930.

It would be untruthful to say that Baverstock's time at Hinton Martel was one of feverish parochial

---

[3] A somewhat uninspiring 1870 re-build in the Gothic style by G R Crickmay consisting of aisled nave, chancel and west tower. The only items to be saved from the former building were the thirteenth century font and a chalice and paten of 1634. Any embellishments would have redeemed its dreariness.

[4] Farmer, p.7.

responsibilities, but in addition to the daily offices, the Mass and parish visiting, he did have the administration of St Joseph's Home to look after. Busy as he was he managed to find time for his writings, producing over the thirty-one years of his vicariate twenty-nine pamphlets and a multitude of articles for journals of various Catholic Societies. He also found time to establish the Catholic Literature Association, later renamed as the Church Literature Association.

Though in a rural parish, Fr Baverstock was far from isolated from the events of the wider Catholic movement. A member of the Society of the Holy Cross (SSC) since 1897 he was for many years a member of its Council and served as Master between 1921–24 and again in 1927–29. He was a staunch supporter of corporate reunion, defending the use of the Roman Catholic Latin Breviary and the Roman Missal and wrote on the subject in *The Truth About the Prayer Book* (1935). Throughout his life Fr Baverstock had a life-long devotion to Our Lady and belonged to many Marian societies. In 1931 he became one of the foundation Guardians of the Shrine of Our Lady at Walsingham, and also served as Chaplain-General of the Society of Mary between 1935 and 1944.

In his retirement years Fr Baverstock spent two years as Priest-Director of the Holy Family Homes (who by that time had taken over the administration of St Joseph's), then in 1932 moved to Basingstoke as Chaplain to the Sisters of the Transfiguration. Another move, in 1933, saw him as honorary assistant priest at Holy Trinity, Reading and in 1934 became stipendary curate in the parish. Resigning from his post at Reading in 1938 due to difficulties with the incumbent, Fr Francis Judd, Baverstock took a job in the Civil Service before being offered the Chaplaincy of the Radcliffe Infirmary, Oxford, a post he held until his retirement in 1946. For the next four years he lived quietly in Reading, being looked after by his housekeeper, contributing articles and book reviews to various journals. Fr Baverstock celebrated his Golden Jubilee as priest at Hinton Martel in December 1946; it was to be his last living memory of the church, but not his last association. Three years later, on 25th April 1950, he died at home in Reading and, according to his wishes, his body was taken to Hinton Martel for the Solemn Requiem and burial.

How to use this book

Now reissued as *The Eucharistic Year: Seasonal Devotions for the Sacrament*, Fr Baverstock's compilation remains as vibrant today as it did seventy years ago. It is a book to use as an aid to devotion rather than to shelve as an antiquarian relic of the Catholic Days of 1930s Anglicanism. Use it in your prayers before Mass, or as a thanksgiving after receiving the Blessed Sacrament. Here can be found words of wisdom, love, hope and reassurance. The words within it can never grow old, and they remain as true today as they did when compiled in the patristic period. As Fr Baverstock said in his Preface, 'We are in the same world of ideas; there is the same loving devotion to him, who, having given himself for us on Calvary, gives no less than himself to us at the Altar.'

> Draw nigh, and take the body of the Lord,
> And drink the holy blood for you outpoured,
> Saved by that bread, hallowed by that blood,
> Whereby refreshed we render thanks to God.

Latin, 7th century
Tr. John Mason Neale

Julian W S Litten
Walthamstow 2001

DEDICATED TO ALL
DEVOUT COMMUNICANTS

ADVENT I.

I. 3RD CENT. ST. HIPPOLYTUS. *(On the End of the World. Ch. xli.)*

Then shall the divine Judge say to those on his right hand : Come, ye blessed of my Father. Come, ye Patriarchs, who before mine Advent served me and longed for the coming of my Kingdom. Come, ye Apostles, partakers of my afflictions for the Gospel's sake. Come, ye martyrs, who confessed me before tyrants and endured many sore punishments and tortures. Come, ye Prelates, who made me a pure oblation and daily offered my precious Body and Blood.

II. 5TH CENT. ST. CHRYSOSTOM. *(Hom. iii. on Ephes. i.)*

Consider what care and diligence they shewed who took part in the ancient sacrifices. How they gave themselves ever to cleansing and expiation. But thou drawest nigh to that Victim whom the very Angels worship in awe and wonder. How shalt thou stand at the judgment seat of Christ, if thou darest to approach his very Body with hands and lips polluted? Thou wouldest not dare to kiss the feet of a king with a mouth reeking of foulness. Yet with a foul and reeking soul dost thou kiss the King of heaven. A monstrous wrong.

III. 4TH CENT. ST. CYRIL OF JERUSALEM. *(Cat. iv.)*

Look not upon the eucharistic bread and wine as bare and common elements. For they are Christ's Body and Blood according to the Lord's declaration.

1

For although the sense suggest the former, yet faith should make thee firm and sure of the latter. Judge not the matter from taste, but by faith be thou sure beyond all doubt that thou art granted the gift of Christ's Body and Blood.

IV. 5TH CENT. ST. SALVIAN OF MARSEILLES. *(To the Catholic Church, Bk. ii.)*

The Jews of old had the shadow of things, we the truth. To the Jews a servant was sent to be their master, to us the Son. The Jews ate manna, we Christ; the Jews the flesh of sheep, we the Body of Christ; the Jews what was rained down from heaven, we the God of heaven.

V. 7TH CENT. ST. ISIDORE OF SPAIN. *(Against the Jews, Bk. ii.)*

The Wisdom of God, even Christ, hath furnished a table, to wit the Altar of the Lord, saying: Come, eat of my Bread, and drink of the Wine which I have mingled for you: that is, take the food of the holy Body and drink the Cup of the sacred Blood.

VI. 4TH CENT. ST. EPHRAEM. *(Sermon against Questioners.)*

Receive the sinless Body and Blood of thy Lord in fullest faith, assured that thou feedest upon the Lamb himself in his entirety.

VII. 4TH CENT. ST. EPHRAEM. *(Sermon i. on the Most Holy Christian Sacraments.)*

Since the word of God is living and operative, and God created all things which he willed to create, in such wise that when he said, Let there be light, the

2

light was straightway made, and when he said, Let there be a firmament, it was so, and, above all, since God willed that the Word should be born as man, how then, I ask you, should not the Word of God himself be able to make Bread become the Body of Christ, and Wine his Blood?

ADVENT II.

I. 4TH CENT. ST. AMBROSE. *(Book on the Mysteries. Ch. ix.)*

If the word of Elijah had power to bring down fire from heaven, shall not the word of Christ have power to change the character of the elements? But what need have we of arguments? Let us take our Lord himself as an example, and prove the truth of the Mystery by the mystery of the Incarnation. We know that the Virgin gave him birth beyond the order of nature. And this that we make by consecration is the Body born of a Virgin. Why seekest thou here the order of nature in the matter of Christ's Body, seeing that beyond nature the Lord Jesus was born of a Virgin?

II. 5TH CENT. ST. JEROME. *(Commentary on St. Matt. xxvi.)*

After the typical Passover had been fulfilled and Christ had eaten with his Apostles the flesh of a Lamb, he takes bread and passes on to the true Passover Sacrament, that as Melchizedek had done of old in a figure, offering bread and wine, he himself might show forth the truth of his Body and Blood.

III. 5TH CENT. ST. CHRYSOSTOM. *(Exposition of Ps. cxliv.)*

A son glorifieth his father (Mal. i.). Thou art made a son, and thou enjoyest a spiritual table, eating the Flesh and Blood of him who regenerated thee. Give thanks therefore for so great a benefit, and render glory and honour to him from whom thou receivest it.

IV. 4TH CENT. COUNCIL OF NICÆA.

We believe in his Son Jesus Christ, the Word of
God, begotten of the Father before all worlds, and
sent by God the Father into the world : who made
his abode in Mary the Virgin and took flesh of her,
whereby he hid from mortals the majesty of his
Godhead; who is herein perfect God and perfect
man, who by grace bestowed upon men the eucharistic Bread and holy Wine, the Food of Angels, to
wit his very Flesh and his very Blood, saying : This
is my Blood of the new and holy testament, which I
have given to you.   As often, therefore, as ye eat
and drink thereof, do this in remembrance of me.

V. 5TH CENT. ST. CYRIL OF ALEXANDRIA. *(Bk. xiii.*
Of worship in spirit and in truth.)

We eat the Bread which is from heaven, to wit
Christ, who was made like unto us. But Christ both
was and is God, coming from above, from the Father,
and he is King and Lord above all, over all things.

VI. 6TH CENT. ST. REMIGIUS OF RHEIMS. *(Com-*
mentary on 1 Cor. x.)

The flesh which the Word of God the Father took
in the Virgin's womb, united to his Person, and the
Bread which is consecrated in the Church, are the
One Body of Christ.   For as that flesh is the Body
of Christ, so this Bread becometh the Body of
Christ.

VII. 8TH CENT. ST. ETHERIUS. *(Bk. i. Against*
Elipandus.)

We eat his Body and drink his Blood, that as it
passeth visibly into our inward parts, so we may be
inwardly united to him and transformed.   For it is
a sacrament and a mystery.

5

ADVENT III.

I. 5TH CENT. ST. AUGUSTINE. *(Treatise ii. on St. John iii.)*

The faithful receive manna, having already passed through the Red Sea. That sea signified Christ's baptism. Whither then doth he lead them that believe and are baptised? To the Manna. Mark my words, to the Manna. It is known what the Jews received. But Catechumens do not know what Christians receive. Let them blush to be ignorant, let them pass through the Red Sea and eat this Manna, that as they have believed in the Name of Jesus, so Jesus may commit himself unto them.

II. 6TH CENT. PRIMASIUS OF AFRICA. *(Commentary on Rev. ii.)*

To him that overcometh will I give of that hidden Manna, that is, of the invisible Bread which came down from heaven. For he was made man that man might eat the Bread of Angels.

III. 4TH CENT. ST. AMBROSE. *(Bk. i. On St. Luke i. 11.)* " There appeared unto him an angel."

Doubt not that the Angel standeth by when Christ is there, when Christ is offered in sacrifice.

IV. 5TH CENT. ST. CHRYSOSTOM. *(Bk. iii. On the Priesthood.)*

Angels stand by the priest: the whole order of Virtues crieth out: all the space about the altar is filled with these heavenly powers, in honour of him who lieth thereon.

6

V. 7TH CENT. ST. GREGORY THE GREAT. *(Sacra-
    mentary. Preface for 5th Sunday after
    Epiphany.)*

Christ's Body is made by the operation of the
Holy Ghost. Each receiveth Christ the Lord, and
in each portion he is entire.

VI. 4TH CENT. ST. JAMES NISIBIS. *(Sermon iii.
    On Fasting.)*

One door there is of thy house: and that house
is the temple of God. Wherefore it is wrong and
altogether unseemly, O man, that through the door
whereby the King entereth in, thou shouldest bring
forth filth and nastiness, but rather that thou
shouldest abstain from all uncleanness, and then
shouldest take the Body and Blood of Christ, and
carefully guard thy mouth, whereby the King
entereth: never more is it allowed thee, O man, to
utter from thy mouth words of uncleanness.

VII. 3RD CENT. ST. IRENAEUS. *(Bk. iv. Against
    Heresies. Ch. xvii.)*

Christ took what was by nature bread, and gave
thanks, saying: This is my Body. And the cup
likewise he proclaimed his Blood; and so taught the
new Oblation of the New Testament, which the
Church, receiving it from the Apostles, offers
throughout the world to God.

ADVENT IV.

I. 7TH CENT. ST. ISIDORE OF SPAIN. *(On 1 Sam. ii. 36.)*

He asketh that in the priest's office he may eat a morsel of bread. By these words the sacrifice of Christians is meetly set forth, concerning which our Priest himself saith : The Bread which I will give you is my Flesh, which I will give for the life of the world. For this is the Sacrifice, not according to Aaron, but according to Melchizedek.

II. 5TH CENT. THEODORET. *(Commentary on Ps. xxxvi.)*

They shall be satisfied with the plenteousness of thy house : and thou shalt give them drink of thy pleasures as out of a river. By these words we understand not only the stream of heavenly doctrine, but also the receiving of the mystic Food.

III. 4TH CENT. EUSEBIUS OF EMISSA. *(Homily for Easter Monday.)*

Let each one take a lamb : and the lamb shall be without blemish. Christ is the Lamb : for of him it is said, Behold the Lamb, that taketh away the sins of the world. And he is the Lamb without blemish, since of him it is written : Who did no sin, neither is guile found in his lips. And this lamb is eaten in the houses; whereby is plainly designated the Sacrifice which to-day is taken in the Church.

IV. 5TH CENT. ST. CHRYSOSTOM. *(Homily xxv. on St. Matthew.)*

What was to God of all things most precious, even his only-begotten Son, he gave for us his enemies: and not only gave him for us, but also set him for us upon the Holy Table.

V. 6TH CENT. ST. CAESARIUS OF ARLES. *(Homily vii. Concerning Easter.)*

And because our Lord was going to take from our sight the body he had taken, and raise it to heaven, it was necessary that he should consecrate for us the Sacrament of his Body and Blood, that through this Mystery that might be celebrated, which once was offered for our price: that as our redemption had daily force for man's salvation, there should be a perpetual oblation thereof. Unique and perfect is our Sacrifice, to be weighed by faith, not by appearance; to be reckoned not by exterior vision, but by inward contemplation.

VI. 6TH CENT. ST. FULGENTIUS. *(Sermon i. on the Nativity of our Lord.)*

That man might eat the Bread of Angels, the Creator of Angels was made man, who feeds both Angels and men and abides entire.

VII. 4TH CENT. ST. GREGORY OF NYSSA. *(Orat. Catech. Ch. xxxvii.)*

I believe that the bread which is sanctified by the Word of God is changed into the Body of the Word of God.

9

B

CHRISTMAS.

I. 5TH CENT. ST. MAXIMUS. *(Homily v. on the Nativity of our Lord.)*

To-day was Christ born for us in the flesh, as we learned from the gospel reading. He is wrapped in swaddling bands and laid in the manger. This poverty of the Infant is a precious mystery of God; for in his swaddling bands he shows that he has taken upon him our infirmities, our sins. And in that he suffers his limbs to be laid in a manger, where beasts feed, he shows that his Body shall be for the feeding of mortal men to their eternal refreshment.

II. 5TH CENT. ST. CHRYSOSTOM. *(Homily on St. Philogonius.)*

This Table taketh the place of the manger wherein Christ was born. For here also is set the Body of the Lord, not wrapped indeed in swaddling bands, but compassed around by the Holy Ghost.

III. 7TH CENT. ST. ELIGIUS. *(Homily viii. on the Lord's Supper.)*

As Christ in very truth took our flesh, and very Man, Jesus born of Mary the Virgin, is Son of God, even so it is his true Flesh and his very Blood which we take to eat and drink in the Mystery.

IV. 3RD CENT. ST. ZENO OF VERONA. *(Sermon iv. on the Feast of the Lord's Nativity.)*

O new order ! God compelled by love for his own image becomes an infant, and suffers himself to be bound in swaddling bands, having come to pay the debts of all the world. In a manger in a stable is he laid, witnessing that he is both the Shepherd and the Food of the nations.

V. 5TH CENT. ST. ELEUTHERIUS. *(Sermon on the Lord's Birth.)*

Meet it is that he who was the living Bread should be cradled between two beasts. For this is he who said, I am the living Bread which came down from heaven. This is that pure Lamb whose spotless Body, handled by the priest, eaten by all the faithful, remaineth unharmed and unconsumed.

VI. 5TH CENT. ST. AUGUSTINE. *(Sermon cxc. on the Lord's Nativity.)*

Who is this Infant? Infant, he is called, that is, *in-fans*, one who cannot speak. So then he is both speechless Infant and Word of God. In the flesh he is silent; he teaches through Angels. To the Shepherds is announced the Chief Shepherd, the Shepherd of Shepherds, and in the manger lies the Food of the faithful.

VII. 4TH CENT. ST. CYRIL OF JERUSALEM. *(Catech. iv.)*

In all certainty let us take the Body and Blood of Christ. For under the appearance of bread is given there the Body, and under the appearance of wine is given there the Blood, that receiving the Body and Blood of Christ thou mayest be made of one body and one blood with him. For so shall we be Christophers, that is, men who bear Christ, since we shall have received into our bodies his Body and Blood, and thus shall we be made, as Blessed Peter saith, partakers of the divine nature.

11

VIII. 6TH CENT. ST. LEANDER OF SPAIN. *(On the Institution of Virgins. Ch. vii.)*

The sacrifices of beasts were done away, for they were figures of the true Sacrifice, Christ's Body and Blood. The Truth is come, the shadow goeth. The true Sacrifice is come, the sacrifice of beasts is gone.

IX. 3RD CENT. ST. CYPRIAN. *(Epistle lxiii. to Cecilius.)*

Our Lord Jesus Christ is supremely the Priest of the Most High God, who offered Sacrifice to God the Father. And he offered the sacrifice which Melchizedek had offered, bread and wine, to wit his own Body and Blood.

X. 4TH CENT. JAMES OF EDESSA. *(Chap. xxi. Explanation of Genesis.)*

From the testimony of the holy writers we learn that Melchizedek, in offering sacrifice, departed from the accustomed manner of the Gentiles. For in his sacrifice he used not the flesh and blood of beasts, but was wont to make his offering to the true God with bread and wine, whereby he marvellously showed a type of our spiritual and reasonable and bloodless sacrifice of the Body and Blood of Christ.

XI. 4TH CENT. ST. AMBROSE. *(Bk. ii. Exposition of St. Luke ii.)*

He who would depart in peace, let him come to the temple, let him expect the Lord's Christ; let him receive into his hands the Word of God and embrace him with the arms of faith; then shall he depart in peace, not to see death, since he hath seen the Life.

XII. 5TH CENT. ST. AUGUSTINE. *(On Ps. xxxiii.* [*Vulg.*]*)*

Christ bore himself in his own hands when he gave his very Body, saying, This is my Body. He bore his own Body then in his hands.

EPIPHANY.

I. 5TH CENT. ST. CHRYSOSTOM. *(Homily vii. on St. Matthew.)*

Hasten to Bethlehem, the House of spiritual Bread, if only thou drawest nigh to honour and adore, and not to trample under foot the Son of God. Beware that thou be not like Herod and say, "That I may come and worship him also," and coming, seek to slay him. For they who are partakers of the mysteries unworthily are like Herod. Let us fear then, lest, presenting the appearance of suppliant worshippers, we contradict our appearance by our acts.

II. 3RD CENT. ST. CYPRIAN. *(Sermon on the Lord's Supper.)*

Of this Bread, the manna which fell in the desert was a type. This is the Bread of Angels, serving to the appetite of all who worthily and devoutly eat thereof, tempering itself to their liking.

III. 4TH CENT. EUSEBIUS OF EMISSA. *(Homily v. concerning Easter.)*

When thou drawest nigh to the holy altar to be refreshed with saving meat and drink, look with faith upon the Sacred Body and Blood of thy God, adore in wonder, grasp him with thy mind, hold him in thy heart, and feed on him inwardly.

IV. 5TH CENT. ST. CHRYSOSTOM. *(Against the Anomaeans. Homily vi.)*

The Feast of Epiphany is the feast of all feasts to be had in highest honour. If we draw nigh with faith, we shall without doubt behold him lying in the manger, for this holy table takes the manger's place. Those who have been initiated into the holy mysteries understand what I say. The Magi only worshipped him. But to thee, if thou come with a pure conscience, it is permitted to receive him and take him home with thee.

V. 5TH CENT. THEODOTUS OF ANCYRA. *(Homily on the Birth of Christ read at the Council of Ephesus.)*

He who then by his wondrous power drew the Magi to adore him, hath to-day ordained this joyful feast. No longer is he set in the manger, but he is set upon this Altar of salvation. He is set thereon that he may be eaten thereon, and become to the faithful the food of salvation.

VI. 5TH CENT. ST. CHRYSOSTOM. *(Homily xxiv. on 1 Cor. x.)*

This Body hath Christ given us both to take and to eat, in his wondrous love. Let us draw near, therefore, to him with fervour and with burning love. This Body, lying in the manger, the Magi venerated. They travelled from afar, and coming with fear and much trembling, worshipped it. Thou beholdest him not in the manger, but on the Altar. Let us show far greater reverence than those barbarian men.

VII. 5TH CENT. COUNCIL OF ARLES. *(Canon xv.)*

The deacon may not sit among the priests in the sacristy; nor may he presume to give the Body of Christ when a priest is present.

VIII.　2ND CENT.　ST. IGNATIUS OF ANTIOCH.
(Epistle to the Ephesians.)

Obey the Bishop and the priesthood with unswerving mind, breaking One Bread, which is the medicine of immortality, the antidote, that we die not but ever live in the Lord.

EPIPHANY I.

I. 5TH CENT. THEODORET. *(Quaest. xxvii. on Exodus [on 1 Cor. x. 1, etc.].)*

Moses was a type of Christ our Saviour; the manna, of the heavenly Food; the water from the rock, of the saving Blood. For as the Children of Israel, after they had crossed the Red Sea, were given a strange food and water beyond expectation, even so we, after saving baptism, are made partakers of the holy mysteries.

II. 8TH CENT. ST. JOHN OF DAMASCUS. *(Bk. iv. on the Orthodox Faith. Ch. xiii.)*

Since it was the custom of men to wash with water and anoint themselves with oil, Christ, in baptism, coupled the grace of the Spirit with oil and water. Similarly, because it was men's wont and custom to eat bread and to drink wine and water, he conjoined his divinity with these elements and made them his Body and Blood.

III. 5TH CENT. ST. AUGUSTINE. *(Sermon cxciv. on the Birth of our Lord.)*

The Word was made Flesh and dwelt among us. That man might eat the Bread of Angels, the Creator of Angels was made man.

IV. 4TH CENT. ST. SILVESTER. *(Sermon on the Lord's Temptation.)*

He who in paradise had won the victory over Adam, in the wilderness tempted the Lord. He had

17

conquered Adam when he ate, he must needs be conquered by our Lord while he fasted. And as from Adam's eating, by the counsel of the devil, all who are born are condemned to death, even so by the Lord's fasting all those who are born again attain life everlasting. As death is the lot of those who are born of Adam's flesh and blood, so life is the inheritance of those who are born again of water and the Holy Ghost and have imparted to them the Body and Blood of Jesus Christ our Lord.

V. 5TH CENT. ST. CHRYSOSTOM. *(On Ps. xxiii.)*

Thou hast prepared a table for me against them that trouble me. Who are these that trouble me? Suggestions of the enemy, agitations, lusts, the world's honours. But at the table of the ruler, tribulations become consolations.

VI. 6TH CENT. ST. JOHN CLIMACUS. *(xxiiird Step of the Ascent to Paradise.)*

At the sacred Synaxis, at the very time when the awful mystery of the Eucharist is being transacted, a horrible blasphemy is wont to attack the Lord from impious thoughts, profaning the Sacrifice itself, whence we clearly gather that these unspeakable and accursed thoughts against God come, not from our soul, but from the devil, God's enemy. For if these foul and evil words formed in the mind are mine, how is it that, receiving the heavenly gift, I suppliant adore? He who is troubled by this spirit of blasphemy and longs to be delivered therefrom, let him know that thoughts of this kind spring, not from his soul, but from that same impure devil who said of old to the Lord, All these things will I give thee, if thou wilt fall down and worship me. Let us then

18

despise him and care not at all for his phantasms, but say, Get thee behind me, Satan. I will worship the Lord my God.

VII. 7TH CENT. ST. ISIDORE OF SPAIN. *(Bk. i. on the Offices of the Church. Ch. xviii.)*

The disciples did not at first receive the Body and Blood of the Lord fasting. But now by the whole Church it is received fasting.

EPIPHANY II.

I. 4TH CENT. ST. GREGORY NAZIANZEN. *(Orat. iii.)*

Through the bloodless Sacrifice we have communion with Christ, with his Passion and his Godhead.

II. 4TH CENT. OPTATUS OF MILAN. *(Bk. vi. against the Donatists.)*

What is such sacrilege as to break the Altars of God, whereon ye yourselves have offered in times past? What else is the Altar, but the throne of the Body and Blood of Christ?

III. 5TH CENT. ST. AUGUSTINE. *(Tractate xxxix. on the Psalms.)*

Sacrifice and offering thou wouldest not, saith the Psalm to God. Wherefore willed he them no longer? Wherefore willed he them at first? Because all those things were words of promise. When that which was promised was given, the words of promise are taken away; the things that fulfil the promise are given. Those ancient sacrifices, then, as words promissive, are taken away. What is given in fulfilment? The Body which ye know.

IV. 6TH CENT. ST. REMIGIUS OF RHEIMS. *(On 1 Cor. xi.)*

Christ is sacrificed and eaten; and yet abideth living. Bread is offered to God which, although it appeareth to be bread, is the Body of Christ. For

our Lord and Redeemer, taking thought for our
frailty, gave us this Sacrament, that since he cannot
die again and we daily sin, we may have a true sacrifice wherewith we may be enabled to make expiation.

V. 5TH CENT. GELASIUS OF CYZICUS. *(On the
Eucharist.)*

At the divine table let us not stoop to fix attention
on the bread and cup set forth; but by faith let us
understand that on that sacred table is set the Lamb
of God who taketh away the sins of the world,
offered by the priests without shedding of blood.
And verily receiving his precious Body and Blood
let us believe that these are the symbols of our
resurrection.

VI. 6TH CENT. ST. CAESARIUS OF ARLES. *(Hom.
ii. for Easter Day.)*

Christ died for our sins. This is that Lamb which
we are bidden by the Law to eat in one house. What
means this, in one house? In the unity of the Church
are we bidden to eat his Flesh. Needs therefore
must we feed on the Flesh of this our Lamb, with
our loins girt, that is our carnal passions mortified,
with all purity of heart and body.

VII. 4TH CENT. ST. GAUDENTIUS. *(Tractate ii.
to Neophytes.)*

The Creator and Lord of nature, who bringeth
forth bread from the earth, from bread again (as
he can and as he promised) maketh his own Body:
and he who made wine from water, maketh from
wine his own Blood.

21

EPIPHANY III.

I. 4TH CENT. ST. CYRIL OF JERUSALEM. *(Catech. iv.)*

Christ of old changed water into wine, which is something like blood, at Cana of Galilee, by his will alone. Is he not worthy of our belief, that he hath changed wine into Blood? For if he wrought this wondrous miracle when he was invited to earthly nuptials, shall we not far more readily acknowledge that he hath given his Body and Blood to the children of his Bride?

II. 5TH CENT. ST. JEROME. *(Apologia to Jovinian.)*

I know that at Rome the custom prevails of the faithful daily receiving Christ's Body. I neither blame nor approve the custom. Let a man examine himself and so draw near to the Body of Christ, not thinking that one or two days of deferred communion will make him a holier Christian, so as to be fit to-morrow or the day after when he is not fit to-day.

III. 5TH CENT. ST. EUCHERIUS. *(On Genesis. Bk. ii. Ch. xviii.)*

Christ came, as Man among men, but not of sacerdotal lineage. He was not, that is, of the tribe of Levi, but of Judah, a tribe which gave him no sacerdotal precept. And this on account of the sacramental mystery which Christians are enjoined to celebrate, that we should not offer beasts as victims, according to the priesthood of Aaron, but should offer the oblation of bread and wine, that is, the Sacrament of his Body and Blood, for our Sacrifice.

IV. 4TH CENT. COUNCIL OF NICÆA. *(Ch. xix.)*

If any of the lapsed should come to the point of death while he is under penance, he is not to be deprived of Holy Communion, if he ask for it.

V. 5TH CENT. ST. ISIDORE OF PELUSIUM. *(Bk. ii. Epistle lii.)*

A divine thing is priesthood, of all things the most honourable. Wherefore let those who belittle priesthood cease so to do, lest they sharpen the avenging sword of God against them. Let them rather celebrate it with praises; for by its means we are both regenerated and made partakers of the divine mysteries, without which no one can attain the heavenly rewards, as is evident from the oracles of the Truth himself who first used these words: Except a man eat my Flesh, etc. Wherefore if without these mysteries we cannot attain the eternal abode, and they are only celebrated through the priesthood, surely he who despises the priesthood insults what is divine. That this may not happen let us esteem the priesthood as a thing divine.

VI. 5TH CENT. ST. CHRYSOSTOM. *(On Ps. cxxxiv.)*

Ye that stand in the house of the Lord, even in the courts of the house of our God. Consider what purity is rightly to be demanded of thee. For not Cherubim, but the Lord of the very Cherubim hast thou dwelling in that house; not the urn, the manna, the tables of stone and Aaron's rod, but the Lord's Body and Blood.

VII. 3RD CENT. ORIGEN. *(Homily xv. on sundry passages in the Gospels.)*

When thou receivest the holy Food, the banquet incorrupt, the Bread of life and the cup, thou dost

23

eat and drink the Body and Blood of the Lord. Then doth the Lord come under thy roof. Do thou then, humbling thyself, imitate the centurion and say, Lord, I am not worthy that thou shouldest come under my roof.

EPIPHANY IV.

I. 4TH CENT. EUSEBIUS OF EMISSA. *(Homily on Gospel for 3rd Sunday after Epiphany.)*

When we draw nigh to Christ's Sacrament, and consider our own frailty, what else doth each one of us say but, I am not worthy that thou shouldest come under my roof : I am not worthy to receive thy Body and Blood in my mouth.

II. 5TH CENT. ST. CHRYSOLOGUS OF RAVENNA. *(Sermon cxcii. on the Centurion.)*

I am not worthy that thou shouldest come under my roof. Brethren, this roof is the body, which houses the soul, which veils the domicile of the heart. Beneath this roof the centurion holds it not meet that Christ should enter, that is, that the divine Majesty should enter a human body. But God, who, at his will, can make what is human to be divine, disdains not to dwell in Flesh, nor to enter under the roof of our body.

III. 5TH CENT. ST. CHRYSOSTOM. *(Homily ii. on 2 Tim. i.)*

The oblation which Christ gave to his disciples, and that which priests offer to-day are one and the same. This is no less than that. For as the words which God then spoke are the same words which the priest now speaks, so is this oblation one and the same. It was the Body of Christ then : it is the Body of Christ now. If anyone think our offering is less than his was, it is only because he is ignorant that Christ is present and works among us.

25

IV. 6TH CENT. ST. CAESARIUS OF ARLES. *(Homily vii. on Easter.)*

When the creatures are set upon our holy altars to be blessed with heavenly words, before they are consecrated by the invocation of the holy name, the substance there is of bread and wine; but after the words of Christ they are the Body and Blood of Christ. What wonder is it if he can change by his word the things which by his word he was able to create?

V. 5TH CENT. ST. AUGUSTINE. *(Tractate l. on St. John xii.)*

If thou art good, thou hast Christ both now and in the time to come. Now by faith, now by the sign of Christ, now by the Sacrament of Baptism, now by the Food and Drink of the altar; thou hast Christ in this present time. But thou shalt have him always, for when thou goest hence, thou shalt come to him. But if thou livest evilly, thou seeemest to have Christ in this present time, for thou enterest into the Church, thou signest thyself with Christ's sign, thou goest to Christ's altar : in this present time thou hast Christ; but by reason of thine evil life thou shalt not have him always.

VI. 5TH CENT. ST. CHRYSOSTOM. *(Homily iii. on Ephesians.)*

Reflect that this is his Body and Blood who sitteth above the heavens, who is suppliantly adored by Angels.

VII. 5TH CENT. ST. JEROME. *(Commentary on Ps. lxxviii.)*

While the meat was yet in their mouths, the heavy wrath of God came upon them. And now in the

Church, if any man be refreshed with the Body and Blood of Christ and turn aside to wickedness, let him know that the vengeance of God hangs over him.

EPIPHANY V.

I. 5TH CENT. ST. CHRYSOLOGUS OF RAVENNA.
(Sermon lxviii. on the Lord's Prayer.)

Give us this day our daily bread. Daily he wills
that in the sacrament of his Body we should ask for
our viaticum of bread, that thereby we may come to
the eternal day, and to Christ's altar : that what we
have tasted here we may hereafter receive in fulness
to our utter satisfaction thereby.

II. 5TH CENT. ST. JEROME. *(Bk. ii. To Jovinian.)*

There is one sanctification in the mysteries, for
lord and servant, for noble and ignoble, for king
and common soldier.

III. 6TH CENT. PRIMASIUS OF AFRICA. *(Commentary on 1 Cor. x.)*

All things which were done in figure for the people
of Israel, for us are realised in truth. They did eat
spiritual meat, the manna as a type of the Body of
Christ.

IV. 6TH CENT. ST. FULGENTIUS. *(Bk. viii. against Fabian.)*

Holy Church, when in the sacrifice of the Body
and Blood of Christ she prays that the Holy Spirit
may be sent her, asks for the gift of Charity, whereby she may be able to keep the unity of the Spirit in
the bond of peace.

V. 4TH CENT. EUSEBIUS OF EMISSA. *(Homily on the Gospel for Palm Sunday.)*

My Flesh is meat indeed, and my Blood is drink indeed : and he that eateth me, even he shall live by me. Unless bread and wine were turned into the Body and Blood of Christ, never would he be bodily eaten and drunk. The former are changed into the latter : the latter are eaten and drunk in the former. How this comes to pass, he knoweth who can do all things and knoweth all things.

VI. 5TH CENT. ST. CHRYSOSTOM. *(Homily l. on St. Matthew.)*

Let us not think that it is enough for our salvation, if we offer to the holy Table a chalice of gold studded with jewels. If you wish to honour this Sacrifice, offer your soul, for which Christ was sacrificed; make this golden. It was no golden table, nor gold chalice, at which Christ gave his Blood to his disciples : yet all there were awful and precious, for all were filled with the Spirit. He who said, This is my Body, said also, Inasmuch as ye did it not unto the least of these little ones, ye did it not unto me.

VII. 8TH CENT. ST. GERMANUS OF CONSTANTINOPLE. *(Contemplation of Matters Ecclesiastical.)*

We celebrate with praises the great mystery of the dispensation of the Son of God, incomprehensible, inscrutable, and celebrating it we cry : We offer thee of thine own : of thine own Body and Blood, for thou hast said, Do this in remembrance of me. This it is that we do : what thou hast handed down to us through thy holy Apostles, this we offer to thee for our salvation.

SEPTUAGESIMA.

I. 4TH CENT. ST. AMBROSE. *(On the Mysteries. Ch. ix.)*

That sacrament which thou receivest is made by the word of Christ. Of all the things of the world thou hast read that he spake the word and it was done, he commanded and they were created. Shall not then the word of Christ, which was able to make out of nothing that which was not, be able to change the things that are to that which they were not? For it is a greater thing to give things their natures anew than to change the natures they have.

II. 3RD CENT. ST. CYPRIAN. *(Sermon on the Lord's Supper.)*

When supper was set, ancient forms and new met in the sacramental banquet: the lamb consumed, which the ancient tradition enjoined, the Master set before his disciples a Food that could never be consumed.

III. 4TH CENT. ST. CYRIL OF JERUSALEM. *(Catech. iv.)*

Imbued with most certain faith that that which seemeth bread is not bread, although to be felt as such by the taste, but the Body of Christ; and that that which seemeth to be wine is not wine, although it so appear to the taste, but the Blood of Christ; stablish thine heart.

IV. 5TH CENT. ST. LEO THE GREAT. *(Sermon vii. on the Lord's Passion.)*

That shadows might give place to the body, and that images might cease at the presence of the truth, the ancient observance is abolished by the new sacrament : the victim passes into the Victim, Blood excludes blood, and the feast of the Law, while it is changed, is fulfilled.

V. 4TH CENT. ST. MACARIUS OF EGYPT. *(Homily on the Lord's Nativity.)*

As in Adam all die, even so in Christ shall all be made alive. He is the same in heaven above and in earth below : the Lamb, the Sacrifice, the Victim, the Sacrificing Priest, the True Vine, the Wine that maketh glad, the Treasure, the Warrior, the Victor, the Head of the Church, the Way, the Gate, the Sun of righteousness, the Light of souls, the Life.

VI. 5TH CENT. ST. AUGUSTINE. *(Sermon i. on the Season.)*

In Christ's Body standeth our life, according to his saying, Except ye eat the Flesh of the Son of Man and drink his Blood, ye have not life in you. Let him, therefore, who desires to receive the Life change his life : for if he change not his life, he shall receive the Life unto condemnation. For thus said the Apostle : He that eateth the Body of the Lord and drinketh his Blood unworthily eateth and drinketh damnation to himself.

VII. 5TH CENT. ST. AUGUSTINE. *(Tract. xxvii. on St. John vi.)*

What is it that we believe and are sure of ? That thou art the Christ, the Son of the living God : and in thy Flesh and Blood thou givest only what thou art.

SEXAGESIMA.

I. 5TH CENT. THEODORET. *(Commentary on Heb. viii.)*

If the priesthood which is according to the Law is ended, and the Priest also who is according to Melchizedek hath offered his Sacrifice, the other sacrifices should not be needful : why do the priests of the New Testament perform the mystic Liturgy? It is clear to those who are instructed in things divine that we do not offer another sacrifice, but the memorial of that one sacrifice : for this is what the Lord commanded : Do this in remembrance of me.

II. 8TH CENT. ETHERIUS. *(Bk. i. Against Elipandus.)*

The Sacrifice which is offered to God by Christians our Lord Christ first instituted when he gave his Body and Blood to the Apostles, before he was betrayed.

III. 5TH CENT. ST. CHRYSOSTOM. *(Homily xxvii. on 1 Cor. xi.)*

We are guilty of that drunkenness and excess whereof the Corinthians were then accused. And when? Always to some extent, but chiefly on festivals, when least of all should this be. For the drunkenness follows after communion. And after thou hast received the Blood of Christ thou art debauched. When thou hast received spiritual food thou essayest satanic dainties. Consider what the Apostles did, when they had received that sacred banquet; did they not turn to prayer and the singing of hymns? Hast thou not heard how those three thousand men (Acts ii.), who were partakers of Communion, remained stedfast in prayer, not in feasting and drunkenness? It is true thou fastest before receiving that thou mayest seem in some wise worthy of Communion : but when thou hast received, when thou shouldest increase thy temperance, thou losest all. At both times one should be temperate, but chiefly so when thou hast received the Bridegroom : before Communion, that thou mayest be worthy to receive it; after Communion, that thou mayest not seem unworthy of what thou hast received.

IV. 6TH CENT. ST. REMIGIUS OF RHEIMS. *(On 1 Tim. ii. 1.)* " I exhort, therefore, that first of all supplications, prayers, intercessions and giving of thanks be made for all men."

The blessed Apostle, giving these words of direction to Timothy, handed on to all Bishops and Priests in him the form according to which they should celebrate the solemnities of the Mass and pray for all men. This form the whole Church keeps now : for the supplications are all that comes in the Mass before the priest begins to consecrate the mysteries of the Body and Blood of the Lord, when he says : Te igitur, etc.

V. 5TH CENT. ST. AUGUSTINE. *(Letter to Januarius. Bk. i. 5 and 6.)*

It is quite clear that when the disciples first received the Lord's Body and Blood, they did not receive them fasting. Is the universal Church then to be blamed because the Sacrament is always re-

ceived fasting? For it seemed good to the Holy
Ghost that in honour of so great a Sacrament the
Lord's Body should enter the mouth of a Christian
before any other food; and on that account this
custom is observed all over the world.

VI. 5TH CENT. ST. CYRIL OF ALEXANDRIA. *(Bk. xi.*
Of worship in spirit and in truth.)

Holy should the souls be that partake of that holy
food, the Body of Christ.

VII. 4TH CENT. ST. EPHRAEM. *(Funeral prayer*
for a Deacon.)

Bid him, Lord, I pray thee, to be in bliss in thine
abode. Thou didst command him to transmit holy
mysteries in the Sanctuary, to give thy Body and thy
Blood to thy flock: bid, I beseech thee, that he be
called to share the common pasture with thy lambs.

QUINQUAGESIMA.

I. 5TH CENT. ST. CYRIL OF ALEXANDRIA. *(Bk. xi. Ch. xii. Commentary on St. John xvi.)*

I in them, saith the Lord, and thou in me, that they may be made perfect in one. For he is in us the faithful, bodily as man, being commingled and united with us through the mystic Eulogia; spiritually as God. It is plain then that Christ is the bond of our unity with God the Father. Therefore are we made perfect in unity with God the Father by Christ as the medium, by receiving in ourselves both bodily and spiritually him who is by nature and in very truth his Son, who is substantially united with the Father : being made partakers and sharers of the supreme nature we have been glorified.

II. 5TH CENT. SALVIAN OF MARSEILLES. *(Bk. vi. On the guidance of God.)*

I ask of all men's consciences, which place holds the greater number of Christians, the circus for public games, or the place of God's altar? God's temple is despised that men may run to the theatre. The Church is emptied; the circus is filled; we turn our backs on Christ on the altar.

III. 3RD CENT. ST. CYPRIAN. *(Bk. on the public shows.)*

Hastening to the show, leaving the Lord's house and still bearing with him the Eucharist, that unfaithful man bore with him Christ's Body.

35

IV. 5TH CENT. ST. CHRYSOSTOM. *(Homily on the Lord's Birth.)*

Consider with thyself, O man, what Victim thou art asked to receive, what Table about to approach. Consider this also, that thou, being dust and ashes, takest the Body and Blood of Christ.

V. 3RD CENT. ORIGEN. *(On the Psalms.)*

Taste and see that the Lord is gracious. It may be that exhorting to the tasting of Christ the Psalmist by these words pointed to his Body.

VI. 4TH CENT. ST. EPHRAEM. *(Exhortation to the penitent, xxxi.)*

Grant, O Lord, for thy most sacred Body and Blood's sake, which I unworthy have received at the priest's hands, I may attain the pardon which I so deeply desire.

VII. 5TH CENT. ST. AUGUSTINE. *(Confessions. Bk. x. Ch. xliii.)*

The proud shall not have me in derision; for I consider my Price: I eat him and drink him and supplicate him.

LENT I.

I. 5TH CENT. ST. CYRIL OF ALEXANDRIA. *(Sermon on the Mystic Banquet.)*

Christ to-day receiveth us at his feast: in his mercy and loving kindness he refresheth us, he the Lamb of God who taketh away the sins of the world is slain. The Father rejoiceth: the Son of his free will is offered in sacrifice, not to-day by the enemies of God, but by himself, that he may signify that for men's salvation he voluntarily endured torments. O wondrous mystery.

II. 4TH CENT. ST. GREGORY OF NYSSA. *(Homily viii. on the Church.)*

He who is from eternity setteth himself before us for our food that, having received him in ourselves, we may become what he is.

III. 5TH CENT. ST. CHRYSOSTOM. *(Homily iii. on Ephes. i.)*

I see many who are partakers of Christ's Body inconsiderately and rashly, from custom and use rather than from thought and consideration. The holy time of Lent comes, and everyone, regardless of his condition, becomes a partaker of the mysteries. This is not the time for drawing near: Lent does not make men fit to come; only purity of soul does this. With this purity always come, without it, never.

IV. 4TH CENT. ST. EPHRAEM. *(On Leviticus viii.)*

The hallowing of the vesture of the levitical priests by the anointing oil and the blood of victims clearly symbolised the Sacrifice of the New Testament to be offered by priests upon the mystic table, and the Holy Ghost coming down upon it.

V. 4TH CENT. VICTOR OF ANTIOCH. *(Commentary on St. Mark xiv.)*

Peter, by penitence and inward sorrow of soul, obtained not only a sure hope of pardon but full remission of all his sins. By the falls of saints recorded in the divine scriptures we are warned, if we fall as they fell, to a sedulous imitation of their penitence; since a merciful God has left us penitence as the sole remedy of salvation after a fall. This medicine they who call themselves Cathari, or the pure, seek to take from us. Let the Cathari remember that the Apostle Peter, before Christ was taken captive and he thrice denied him, had been a partaker of the Body and precious Blood of our Lord Jesus Christ, and yet he fell: but through penitence he rose again and obtained pardon of his sins.

VI. 5TH CENT. ST. JEROME. *(Letter to Lucinius.)*

You ask about fasting on Saturday and about daily communion. I answer briefly that we should keep the ecclesiastical traditions as they have been handed down to us by those who were before us. With regard to the Eucharist, so long as our conscience is clear, we should always receive it, and hear the voice of the Psalmist: Taste and see that the Lord is gracious.

VII. 5TH CENT. ST. CYRIL OF ALEXANDRIA. *(Sermon on the Mystic Banquet.)*

Let us take the Body of him who is the Life and drink his holy Blood for the remission of sins and the receiving of immortality: believing the while that he abideth both Priest and Victim, that it is he who offers and is offered.

LENT II.

I. 6TH CENT. ST. CAESARIUS OF ARLES. *(Homily vii. on Easter.)*

Heavenly authority assures us, My Flesh is meat indeed, and my Blood is drink indeed. Let all doubtfulness of unbelief depart therefore, since he who is the author of the gift is himself also the witness of its truth.

II. 7TH CENT. ST. ISIDORE OF SPAIN. *(Bk. i. on the Office of the Church. Ch. xviii.)*

There is all the difference between the shew-bread and Christ's Body that there is between the shadow and the substance, the image and the truth, the exemplars of things to come and those things which they prefigured. Therefore certain days should be appointed for which a man should live more carefully that he may be able more worthily to approach so great a sacrament.

III. 4TH CENT. ST. CYRIL OF JERUSALEM. *(Catech. v. on the Sacred Liturgy.)*

You have seen the deacon giving the priest water for the washing of his hands. He did not give it to cleanse bodily stains, not at all. This washing of the hands is a symbol, to show that you should be clean from all sins and prevarications. Have you not heard Blessed David declaring to us the symbol of this mystery, when he saith, I will wash my hands in innocency?

IV. 5TH CENT. ST. CHRYSOSTOM. *(Homily xx. to the People of Antioch.)*

Thou dost not venture to handle the sacred Victim with hands unwashed. Then do not approach with unwashed soul : this is a far more serious matter and involves a sharper punishment.

V. 3RD CENT. ORIGEN. *(Homily xvi. on Numbers.)*

We are said to drink the Blood of Christ not only in the rite of the mysteries, but also when we receive his words, in which standeth our life.

VI. 4TH CENT. EUSEBIUS OF EMISSA. *(Homily ii. on Easter Monday.)*

Let them take of the blood of the lamb and put it on either doorpost (Exod. xii. 7). They put the Blood of the Lamb on either doorpost, who receive it both with their lips and in their heart. But they who receive unworthily, or while receiving it do not believe it to be Christ's Blood, set it on one post alone; and it is of these that the Apostle saith : He that eateth and drinketh unworthily eateth and drinketh damnation to himself. Let us, therefore, taking it both with lips and heart, and believing it to be Christ's Blood, set it on either doorpost, and receive it with body and soul.

VII. 5TH CENT. THEODORET. *(Question xxiv. on Exod. Ch. xii.)*

All these things are oracles of our mysteries. For we, too, anoint with the Blood of our Lamb, not the threshold only, but either doorpost, sanctifying our tongue and lips without and our reasonable nature within. And the prescription that that lamb should be eaten in one house, the faithful observe by receiving the divine mysteries in the Church alone.

40

LENT III.

I. 5TH CENT. ST. CHRYSOSTOM. *(Homily ii. to the People of Antioch.)*

He who refused not to pour out his Blood for all men, and who hath imparted to us his Flesh, and again that very Blood, what shall he refuse for our salvation?

II. 5TH CENT. THEODORET. *(On 1 Cor. xi. 29.)*

As Judas betrayed him and the Jews insulted him, so do they treat him with ignominy who with hands unclean take his most holy Body and put it into a mouth impure.

III. 4TH CENT. ST. CYRIL OF JERUSALEM. *(Catech.v.)*

Thou hast heard the voice of him that calleth thee to communion in the holy mysteries and saith : Taste and see that the Lord is gracious. Come then and draw nigh, not with hands outspread, nor with fingers apart, but making thy left hand a throne for thy right, which will receive the King, in the hollow of thy hand take the Body of Christ.

IV. 5TH CENT. ST. CHRYSOSTOM. *(Homily on the Birthday of Christ.)*

When God summoneth thee to his table and setteth his Son there before thee, where the angelic powers stand by in fear and trembling, dost thou dare to come noisily to that spiritual banquet? With awe let us draw near, let us give thanks, let us pour

41

D

out earnest and copious prayers to God, and so cleansing ourselves, in silence and with due modesty, as men coming to the King of heaven, let us draw nigh.

V.   4TH CENT.   ST. GAUDENTIUS.   *(Tractate ii. to Neophytes.)*

Receive this sacrifice with all eagerness of heart, that by our Lord Jesus Christ, whom we believe to be in his mysteries, our inward parts may be sanctified.

VI.   5TH CENT.   ST. CHRYSOLOGUS OF RAVENNA. *(Sermon lxxi. on the Lord's Prayer.)*

Christ himself is the Bread that came down from heaven : daily he comes to the altar for heavenly food, and feeds and nourishes unto eternal life them that eat him.   We pray that this Bread may be given us day by day until we come to enjoy it in the everlasting day.

VII.   6TH CENT.   ST. REMIGIUS OF RHEIMS.   *(On 1 Cor. xi.)*

As that Body which Christ laid upon the cross was sacrificed for our salvation and redemption ; so daily for our salvation and redemption is that Bread offered to God which, although it seem to be bread, is the Body of Christ.

LENT IV.

I. 3RD CENT. ST. CYPRIAN. *(Sermon on the Lord's Supper.)*

As the ordinary bread which we daily eat is the life of the body, so that supersubstantial Bread is the life of the soul and the health of the mind.

II. 8TH CENT. ST. JOHN OF DAMASCUS. *(On the Orthodox Faith. Ch. xiii.)*

Since the Lord himself hath said, My Flesh is meat indeed, etc., and again, He that eateth me, even he shall live by me, therefore let us approach him with all fear, with a pure conscience, and with faith unswerving, let us venerate him with all purity of mind and body. Let us draw near to him with ardent desire, and with our hands disposed crosswise let us receive the Body of the Crucified.

III. 4TH CENT. PHILO OF CARPATHIA. *(Commentary on Cant. viii. 5.)*

I raised thee up under the apple tree. This apple tree of salvation, if thou regardest the tree, is the cross, whereon hung the Creator and Saviour of the world. But if thou lookest rather to the sweet and holy fruit thereof, the all-heavenly and saving fruit is the Body of Christ given us by him for our healing, for meat and for drink, beneath the mystic Bread and Wine, whereby in most holy wise he feeds and blesses all Christians.

43

IV. 6TH CENT. ST. ANASTASIUS OF SINAI. *(Sermon on the Sacred Synaxis.)*

While we assist at the celebration of the holy and awful service, after the consecration of the bloodless sacrifice, the priest holds up on high the Bread of Life, and shows it to all. Then he goes on to say, The holy to the holy. What is this he says? Take heed how ye approach communion in the divine mysteries, lest any one of you coming to communicate should hear the word : Touch me not : depart from me, thou that workest iniquity.

V. 5TH CENT. ST. CHRYSOSTOM. *(Homily v. on Is. vi. " I saw the Lord.")*

When thou art about to approach the holy table, consider that there is present the Lord of all. Yes, he is truly there and he knows what is the mind of each, and he sees who approaches with due holiness, and who with depraved conscience, with unclean and sordid thoughts, with wicked deeds.

VI. 5TH CENT. ST. AUGUSTINE. *(Tractate xxvi. on St. John vi.)*

Before ye come to the altar, consider what it is ye say. Forgive us our trespasses, as we forgive. Thou forgivest? Thou shalt be forgiven : draw nigh assured; it is Bread, not poison. But see if thou dost forgive. For if thou forgivest not, thou liest, and liest to him whom thou canst not deceive.

VII. 5TH CENT. ST. AUGUSTINE. *(On Ps. xxxiv. 5. [Vulg. xxxiii. Draw nigh unto him and be enlightened.])*

He invites us to draw nigh. But let us draw nigh to him that we may be enlightened, not as the Jews

drew near to him, so that they were in darkness.
For they drew near to him to crucify him, we draw
nigh to him to receive his Body and Blood. They
were darkened by his crucifixion : we, eating and
drinking the Crucified, are enlightened.

PASSION WEEK.

I. 4TH CENT. EUSEBIUS OF GAUL. *(Homily on the Story of the Lord's Passion.)*

Jesus, receiving the cup, gave thanks and gave it to them, saying : Drink ye all of this, for this is my Blood, etc. This is my Blood, he saith, which is to be shed. The Blood shed and this Blood are not two different things, but one and the same. To-morrow shall it be shed from my side, to-night ye drink it and behold it in the cup.

II. 5TH CENT. ST. CHRYSOSTOM. *(Sermon on Easter.)*

The thief learned from the flesh the Godhead : from the Body he saw the virtue hidden therein. Imitate the thief, and thou shalt know the Lord. When thou receivest his Body, consider the hidden mystery.

III. 5TH CENT. ST. CYRIL OF ALEXANDRIA. *(Bk. ii. Of worship in spirit and in truth.)*

The death of Christ is the medicine for the undoing of death, and they who are partakers of the mystic Blessing, they be victors over death and destruction, as these words bear witness : Verily I say unto you, he that eateth my Flesh and drinketh my Blood hath eternal life.

IV. 6TH CENT. ST. REMIGIUS OF RHEIMS. *(On 1 Cor. xi.)*

As the Flesh of Christ which he took in the Virgin's womb is his true Body, slain for our salvation; even so the Bread which Christ gave to his disciples and which priests daily consecrate in the Church is Christ's true Body.

V. 4TH CENT. ST. BASIL. *(Rule of Morals xxi.)*

Learn how thou shouldest eat Christ's Body, that is, in memory of Christ's obedience unto death; that they who live should live no longer in themselves, but in him who died for them.

VI. 5TH CENT. THEODORET. *(On Isaiah lxv. As the day of a tree, etc.)*

Of that tree of old God said : Lest Adam stretch out his hand and eat of the tree of life and live for ever. Now to us the saving cross is become the tree of life, and they who hold out their hands, and partake of its Fruit, live a life immortal.

VII. 5TH CENT. ST. PROCLUS OF CONSTANTINOPLE. *(Sermon ii. on Easter.)*

Never did a cross redeem nature from the curse : never was a Lamb set upon the altar that could take away the sins of the world, until God took on him the nature of a servant.

HOLY WEEK.

I. 5TH CENT. ST. AUGUSTINE. *(Against Faustinus. Ch. xviii.)*

The Hebrews with their victims of beasts which they offered to God celebrated the prophecy of the victim to come, offered by Christ on the cross. And now Christians celebrate the memory of this same sacrifice by the most holy oblation and communion of the Body and Blood of Christ.

II. 6TH CENT. ST. FULGENTIUS. *(Letter to Ferrandus. Quest. v. on the Last Supper.)*

In the sacrifice of Christ's Body we begin with thanksgiving to show not that Christ is to be given, but that in very truth he is given to us : by our thanksgiving at the offering of the Body and Blood of Christ we recognise not that Christ is to be slain for our iniquities, but that he hath been slain, not that we are to be redeemed by that Blood, but that we are redeemed.

III. 5TH CENT. ST. CHRYSOSTOM. *(Homily xxiv. on 1 Cor. x.)*

With awe and all purity let us draw nigh. This Body was pierced by the nails, torn by the scourges, yet death took it not from us. This Body nailed to the Cross caused the sun to turn away his rays. And the veil of the temple was rent, the rocks were cleft, and all the earth was shaken. This Body he gave us to hold, in his tender love for us.

IV. 5TH CENT. ST. CHRYSOSTOM. *(On St. John's words:* There came out water and blood.)

Not without cause, not by chance, did these fountains spring forth; for the Church is made by both. This the initiated know. They were regenerated by water, they are fed by Blood and Flesh. The mysteries take their rise here, that often as thou approachest the awful chalice thou mayest so draw nigh as though thou were about to drink from his very side.

V. 4TH CENT. ST. AMBROSE. *(Bk. iv. on the Faith. Ch. x.)*

As often as we receive the sacraments which by the mystery of the holy prayer are transfigured into Christ's Body and Blood, we proclaim the Lord's death.

VI. 4TH CENT. ST. GREGORY OF NYSSA. *(Orat. i. on Easter.)*

Joseph of Arimathæa, when he had received the gift of that immaculate and holy Body, wrapped it in clean linen and laid it in a new and pure tomb. And what this honourable counsellor did, let it be as it were a law for us, that we should do likewise. When we receive the gift of Christ's Body, let us not wrap it in a conscience's dirty linen, nor let us place it in the tomb of a heart full of dead men's bones and all uncleanness.

VII. 5TH CENT. ST. JEROME. *(Commentary on St. Matthew.)*

Receiving his Body, Joseph wrapped it in clean linen. He wraps Jesus in a clean shroud who receives him with a pure heart.

EASTER WEEK.

I. 4TH CENT. ST. EPHRAEM. *(Sermon against Questioners.)*

Hear what the Angels say to the women : the Lord is risen. Believe most firmly that all these things are true as they are told. The eye of faith, when in any man's heart it is clear and bright as the light, purely and sincerely contemplates the Lamb of God, who was slain and sacrificed for us and hath given us his holy and spotless Body that we may feed thereon, and that the partaking of it may be to us for the remission of sins.

II. 5TH CENT. ST. CHRYSOSTOM. *(Homily on the Cemetery.)*

With fear and reverence let us approach. Know ye not how the Angels stood by the sepulchre, when it no longer held the Body, the empty sepulchre? Yet since it had once held the whole Body of the Lord, they show even to the place much honour. Yet we, about to approach, not the empty sepulchre, but the very Table on which the Lamb is set, draw near with tumult. I speak not rashly. It is because I often see many approaching noisily, pushing in each other's way, that I utter this warning.

III. 5TH CENT. ST. AUGUSTINE. *(Sermon ccxxxv. on the days of Easter.)*

When willed the Lord to be recognised? In the breaking of bread. We are safe. We break bread, and we know the Lord. It was only at this point he

chose to be known, for our sakes who should not see
him in the flesh, and yet should eat his Flesh. If
thou wouldest have life, do as they did : in order
to know the Lord they received him in hospitality.
The Lord then showed himself in the breaking of
Bread. Learn where ye may seek the Lord : learn
where ye have him : learn where ye may know him,
when ye eat him.

IV. 3RD CENT. ORIGEN. *(On Ps. xcvii. [Vulg.*
xcviii. " Worship his footstool."])

The footstool some have said to be Christ's Flesh,
which is to be worshipped for Christ's sake. And
Christ is to be adored for the Word of God's sake
which is in him.

V. 4TH CENT. ST. AMBROSE. *(Bk. iii. on the*
Holy Ghost. On the same Psalm.)

By the footstool let earth be understood, and by
earth the Flesh of Christ which to-day we adore in
the mysteries, and which, as we have said, the
Apostles adored in the Lord Jesus.

VI. 5TH CENT. ST. AUGUSTINE. *(Tractate on the*
same Psalm.)

How shall we worship earth, when Scripture
openly saith, Thou shalt worship the Lord thy God?
And here it saith, Worship his footstool. And
showing what is his footstool, it saith, (Is. lxvi. 1),
The earth is my footstool. I am in a doubt. I fear
to worship the earth lest he who made heaven and
earth condemn me. I fear not to adore the footstool
of my Lord, because the Psalm saith : Worship his
footstool. In my doubt I turn me to Christ. It is

him I seek here. And I find how, without impiety,
earth may be worshipped. For he took earth of
earth, since flesh is of earth, and he took flesh of
Mary's flesh. And because in the flesh he walked
here on earth and gave us this very Flesh to be eaten
for our salvation; and no man eateth that Flesh
without first worshipping it : it is found how God's
footstool may be worshipped, and that not only are
we free from sin in worshipping it, but that we sin
if we fail to worship it.

VII. 5TH CENT. ST. ISIDORE OF PELUSIUM. *(Bk. i.*
Epistle cix. Against Macedonius.)

When in the invocation at holy baptism the Holy
Ghost is mentioned together with the Father and the
Son as delivering us from sin, and when at the
mystic Table he makes common bread to be the very
Body of Christ's Incarnation, how canst thou teach
that he is not of one substance with the Father and
the Son?

EASTER I.

I. 5TH CENT. ST. CYRIL OF ALEXANDRIA. *(Exposition of Low Sunday Gospel.)*

And therefore rightly do we keep our holy assemblies throughout the eighth day in the Churches : and we close our doors : and Christ comes and appears to all, in a fashion beyond our seeing, and also in a fashion whereby we may see him : beyond our seeing in his Godhead, but again to be seen in his Body; and he reacheth out his holy Flesh for us to touch and bids us touch it. For by God's gift we draw nigh to receive the mystic Blessing, taking Christ into our hands, that we too may certainly believe that he has raised up his temple.

II. 4TH CENT. ST. AMBROSE. *(Bk. ii. on Penance.)*

As often as reconciliation has been made for sins, we take the Sacrament of the Body, that by his Blood there may be remission of sins.

III. 5TH CENT. ST. CHRYSOSTOM. *(Sermon for Easter.)*

Let soul and body share the mystery. Take the gift in thine hand : take in thy soul that which is hidden therein. Embrace the Bread, and print thy kiss upon the Godhead. Eat the Body, and with thy soul adore what that Body is. Let the hand hold it, and let the soul say : My Lord and my God.

IV. 4TH CENT. ST. EPIPHANIUS. *(On Christ's holy Resurrection.)*

Christ our Passover is sacrificed for us. There is a new people of God, and a new Passover: a new and bloodless sacrifice: a new and divine testament. Of old an heifer is slain for the sins of the people: now for the salvation of the people the Lamb of God is offered in sacrifice. They ate the manna for a season and died: we are fed on the Bread of heaven unto life eternal.

V. 4TH CENT. ST. CYRIL OF JERUSALEM. *(Catech. v.)*

After the communion of the Body of Christ, prepare to receive the cup of his Blood, not reaching out your hands, but prostrate and in the attitude of adoration and worship.

VI. 5TH CENT. ST. CHRYSOSTOM. *(Homily lxxxix. on St. Matthew.)*

Perchance any one of you might wish, like the holy women, to hold the feet of Jesus. But ye can, an ye will, touch not only his feet and his hands but even that sacred head, when with pure conscience ye are partakers of the holy mysteries.

EASTER II.

I. 4TH CENT. VICTOR *(Priest)* OF ANTIOCH. *(Commentary on St. Mark xiv.)*

Take, eat: this is my Body, etc. That the Lord hereby conferred upon the Apostles the power of celebrating the mysteries of the New Testament, I think no one doubts. For to this end he blessed and distributed and bade them take. He did this that from this manner of blessing and giving thanks we may learn how truly great, how worthy of all thanksgiving, are the benefits dispensed to us through Christ's Passion.

II. 4TH CENT. ST. GAUDENTIUS. *(Tract. v. To Neophytes.)*

So shall ye eat it: that is, the lamb: your loins shall be girt up and your shoes on your feet. The true Lamb of God is Christ, on whose Flesh all we the faithful should feed in the mystery, in such wise that our loins be girt in chastity, and our shoes on our feet by the preparation, as the Apostle saith, of the gospel of peace.

III. 5TH CENT. ST. JEROME. *(Commentary on Zech. ix. 17.)*

By the corn of the elect and the wine that maketh virgins, we understand the Lord our Saviour, who saith in the gospel: Except a grain of wheat fall into the ground and die, it abideth alone; but if it die, it bringeth forth more fruit. Of this grain is made that Bread which cometh down from heaven and which strengtheneth man's heart. And he who is the corn of the elect, is also the wine which maketh glad the heart of man.

IV. 4TH CENT. ST. JAMES OF NISIBIS. *(On Judges vii. 5.)*

Great was the mystery, beloved, which God showed before to Gideon, when he bade him separate the men that lapped like dogs. Among all the beasts domestic to man, there is none other that so loves his master and keeps guard over him day and night, as the dog. And even though his master beat him, he leaves him not. Even so, valiant souls, distinguished by these waters, follow their Lord like dogs, and are ready to die for him; they keep their watches and bark against thieves. And they love our Lord: they lick his wounds when they take his Body and put it to their eyes and set their tongue to it.

V. 4TH CENT. ST. PAULINUS OF NOLA. *(Epist. v. to the priest Severus.)*

Christ shall give himself to thee. He is Priest and Sacrifice, Lamb and Shepherd. As Shepherd was he slain for his sheep, and as a Lamb for his shepherds. For the Lord himself is the Victim of all priests, who, offering to the Father for the reconciliation of all, was the Victim of his own Priesthood, and the Priest of his Victim.

VI. 4TH CENT. ST. GREGORY NAZIANZEN. *(Funeral Oration on his sister Gorgonia.)*

She fell down before the altar with faith, and with strong crying called upon him who is honoured thereon.

VII. 5TH CENT. PAULINUS THE DEACON. *(Death of St. Ambrose.)*

Honoratus, a priest of the Church at Vercelli, had laid himself down to rest upstairs, when he heard a voice calling him thrice, and saying: Rise, hasten, for he is now about to depart. So he came down and gave to the Saint the Lord's Body. When he had taken and swallowed it, he gave up the ghost, bearing with him a good *Viaticum*.

EASTER III.

I. 4TH CENT. ST. AMBROSE. *(On Ps. cxix.)*

Come to the food of the Lord's Body, to that cup whereby the soul of the faithful is inebriated, so as to be filled with joy at the remission of sin; and to lay aside the cares of this world, the fear of death, and all anxieties. By this inebriation the body totters not but rises up, the mind is not confused but is consecrated.

II. 5TH CENT. ST. CHROMATIUS OF AQUILEIA. *(On the Lord's Prayer.)*

Let us ask for daily bread, that is, for that heavenly Bread which daily we receive for the healing of the soul and the hope of eternal salvation: of which the Lord saith in the Gospel: The Bread of heaven is my Flesh, which I will give for the life of the world. And this Bread, therefore, we are bidden daily to ask for, that is, that by God's mercy we may be meet daily to receive the Bread of the Lord's Body.

III. 3RD CENT. TERTULLIAN. *(The Resurrection of the Flesh. Ch. viii.)*

The flesh is washed, that the soul may be cleansed: the flesh is anointed, that the soul may be consecrated: the flesh is signed with the cross, that the soul may be defended: the flesh has hands laid upon it, that the soul may be illuminated by the Holy Ghost: the flesh is fed on Christ's Body and Blood, that the soul may be nourished by God.

IV. 4TH CENT. ST. GREGORY OF NYSSA. *(Orat. Catech. Ch. xxxvii.)*

Bread by the word is straightway changed into the Body of the Word, as was said by the Word : This is my Body. The Word of God on this account hath joined himself to the mortal nature of men, that humanity might be deified by communion with Divinity. Therefore, through his Flesh he putteth himself into all that believe, being mingled with the bodies of believers, that by union with that Body which is immortal man might also be a partaker of incorruption.

V. 5TH CENT. THEODORET. *(Commentary on Ps. xxii.)*

The poor shall eat and be satisfied : not all of them, for not all have obeyed the Gospel : but those who have welcomed the love of God towards them. These, as hungry and thirsty, shall, it saith, be filled, enjoying an immortal food. A Food Divine, a doctrine of the Spirit, we know, a mystic and immortal Banquet, familiar to those initiated into the mysteries.

VI. 3RD CENT. TERTULLIAN. *(Baptism. Ch. xvi.)*

He had come by water and by blood, as St. John wrote : to be touched by water, and glorified by Blood; to make us called by water, and elect by Blood. These twain baptisms he sent forth from the wound in his pierced side, that they who believed in his Blood should be washed with water, and they who had been washed with water should drink his Blood. (An allusion to the communion of baptised infants from the chalice.)

VII. 5TH CENT. ST. CHRYSOSTOM. *(On Ps. xlvi.)*

The Jews of old sang a hymn of praise for victory when the host of the Egyptians were drowned in the sea, saying: Sing ye to the Lord, for he hath triumphed gloriously. But far greater is our victory. Instead of the Egyptians drowned, the hosts of Satan overcome: not in the Red Sea, but in the laver of regeneration: not for those going out to the promised land, but for those making their way to heaven: not for men eating manna, but for men feeding on the Lord's Body, drinking, not water from the rock, but Blood from the side.

EASTER IV.

I. 5TH CENT. THEODORET. *(On Ps. lxxxiv.)*

How amiable are thy dwellings. We, too, learn
to say this in view of the benefits we gain from the
altars of God. This word of prophecy indeed
applieth to us more particularly. For it speaks of
many tabernacles, and many altars; whereas the
Jews had but one temple and one altar.

II. 3RD CENT. ST. HIPPOLYTUS. *(On Prov. ix.*
Wisdom hath builded her house, etc.)

Wisdom hath sent out her servants, that is,
Christ hath sent his holy Apostles, going through
the whole world to call the Gentiles by their sublime
and heavenly preaching to the knowledge of him.
Come, eat my Bread and drink the Wine which I
have mingled for you: his own divine Flesh, his
adorable Blood, hath he given us to be eaten and
drunk.

III. 4TH CENT. ST. JAMES OF SARAGOSSA.
(Sermon lxvi. on the Lord's Passion.)

The Lord at the table distributed to them his
Body with his own hands. Hath anybody dared
to deny that it is his Body? Christ himself said:
This is my Body. If any man should deny it, he is
no disciple of the Apostles. The Apostles believed
his words: while he yet lived and was at supper
with them, they fed on him.

IV. 6TH CENT. ST. ANASTASIUS. *(Quest. cxiii. Whether it is right that one going on a journey carry the Eucharist with him.)*

The most holy Body of Christ suffereth no wrong from being carried about. For Christ himself of old went about. Therefore, as I have said, it suffereth no wrong from this, but only from an unclean heart.

V. 4TH CENT. COUNCIL OF NICÆA.

If the Jews boast themselves of the eating of the manna in the desert; you have this greater thing, to wit, the Bread of the Eucharist, which is the Bread of Angels.

VI. 4TH CENT. ST. GREGORY NAZIANZEN. *(Orat. ii. on Easter.)*

Be not disturbed in mind, when thou hearest of the Blood of God, his Passion and his death. Rather, without doubtfulness, eat his Body and drink his Blood, if thou be possessed with the desire of life. Be constant, firm and stedfast, and so disposed as not to waver at all at the talk of heathen adversaries, who make mock of that eating.

VII. 5TH CENT. ST. CYRIL OF ALEXANDRIA. *(On Is. iii.)*

He shall take from Judah the staff of bread. This saying is mystic. For we who by faith have been called to° Christ have a heavenly Bread, that is, Christ, that is, his Body. If anyone ask what is this staff, we reply that it is the staff of life; for he giveth life to the world.

EASTER V.

I. 4TH CENT. PHILO OF CARPATHIA. *(Commentary on Cant. vii.)*

The true ministers of God cleave closely in holiness to the Body and Blood of Christ, as oft as with pure conscience and sincere charity of heart they celebrate aright and handle these divine mysteries.

II. 5TH CENT. ST. CHRYSOSTOM. *(Commentary on Ps. cxli. 3.)*

Consider that the tongue is the member whereby we speak with God and celebrate his praises. With this member we receive the dread Sacrifice. The faithful know what this means. And, therefore, the tongue should be free from all cursing, from every obscene word, every word of calumny.

III. 5TH CENT. ST. CYRIL OF JERUSALEM. *(Catech. v.)*

We entreat God of his mercy to send upon the gifts set forth the Holy Spirit, that he may make the bread Christ's Body and the wine Christ's Blood. For sure it is that whatever the Holy Spirit touches is sanctified and changed.

IV. 4TH CENT. ST. EPHRAEM. *(Sermon against Questioners.)*

Verily it passeth all understanding and all telling what the only-begotten Son of God, Christ our Saviour, hath done for us. Fire and Spirit hath he given us to eat, to wit, his Body and his Blood.

V. 5TH CENT. ST. CHRYSOSTOM. *(Homily ii. to the People of Antioch.)*

Elijah left his mantle to his disciple : the Son of God in his ascension hath left us his Flesh. Elijah put off his mantle to leave it : but Christ hath left us his Flesh and yet hath ascended with it.

VI. 8TH CENT. ST. JOHN OF DAMASCUS. *(Bk. iv. on the Faith. Ch. xiii.)*

The Body is truly united to the Deity, not that the Body which was taken into heaven descends; but that the bread and wine themselves are changed into the Body and Blood of God.

VII. 5TH CENT. THEODORET. *(Commentary on Heb. x.)*

The Veil he calleth the Lord's Flesh : for through it we obtain an entrance into the holy of holies. For as the priest of the old Law entered through the veil into the holy of holies, so they who have believed on the Lord, by partaking of his most holy Body, attain to the heavenly city.

EASTER VI.

I. 3RD CENT. ST. IRENAEUS. *(Bk. iv. against Heresies.)*

For as the bread of earth, receiving the invocation of God, is no longer ordinary bread, but the Eucharist, consisting of two things, earthly and heavenly : so also our bodies, receiving the Eucharist, are no longer corruptible, having the hope of the resurrection.

II. 5TH CENT. ST. CHRYSOSTOM. *(Bk. iii. on Priesthood.)*

The priest should be as pure as if he were set among the angels in heaven. For when thou seest thy Lord sacrificed and lying on the altar, thinkest thou that thou art still among men on the earth? Art thou not rather translated to the heavens, beholding with naked soul, all carnal thoughts laid aside, the things that are in heaven? O miracle! O loving-kindness of God! He who is throned above with the Father, is now held in all men's hands and to all who will giveth himself to be embraced and received.

III. 4TH CENT. ST. PAULINUS OF NOLA. *(Epistle ix. to Severus.)*

The food of our life is Jesus Christ, who was made to be meat for us, that living on that Bread we should be able to say with the Apostle : Our conversation is in heaven.

IV. 5TH CENT. ST. JEROME. *(Commentary on Ps. cx. 4.)*

Thou art a priest for ever after the order of Melchizedek. As Melchizedek the King of Salem

offered bread and wine; so shalt thou offer thy Body
and thy Blood, the true Bread and the true Wine.
This is the Melchizedek who hath given us the
mysteries we have. For he it is who hath said: He
that eateth my Flesh and drinketh my Blood hath
eternal life.

V. 4TH CENT. ST. EPHRAEM. *(Exhortation xix.)*

Let us consider those who stand in the presence of
an earthly king, how in fear they wait upon their
king. Should not we far rather stand in the presence
of our heavenly King with fear and trembling, with
all gravity and reverence? Wherefore I think it not
good with unabashed gaze to contemplate the
mysteries set before us of the Body and Blood of
our Lord and Saviour Jesus Christ.

VI. 4TH CENT. ST. AMBROSE. *(Bk. iv. on the Sacraments. Ch. v.)*

Before it is consecrated, it is bread; but when the
words of Christ have been said, it is the Body of
Christ. And before the words of Christ, the cup is
full of wine and water; but when the words of
Christ have done their work, there is made the Blood
of Christ which redeemed his people. See then in
what sort the word of Christ is mighty to change
all things.

VII. 5TH CENT. ST. CYRIL OF ALEXANDRIA. *(On the Mystic Banquet.)*

Let us contemplate how he who sitteth above the
cherubim yet sitteth at the feast; how he who was
mystically sacrificed in Egypt, here freely offers
himself in sacrifice, himself setting himself before
us as the Food of life.

66

WHITSUNDAY.

I. 5TH CENT. ST. CHRYSOSTOM. *(Homily i. on Pentecost.)*

Unless there were the Holy Ghost, there could not be Pastors and Teachers in the Church. Unless the Holy Ghost had been in the Father and Teacher of you all when a little while ago he gave you all the Peace, you would not all have responded together, And with thy spirit. When he stands at this holy table, about to offer the awful sacrifice (those initiated into the mysteries know what I mean) he waits to take the gifts set forth until he has asked for you grace from the Lord, and until you have replied : And with thy spirit. By this response ye remind yourselves that the celebrant at the altar matters not, but that the power of the Spirit with him effects the mystic sacrifice. For though the priest be but a man, yet is it God who worketh through him.

II. 5TH CENT. ST. CYRIL OF ALEXANDRIA. *(Bk. iii. Commentary on St. John vi.)*

Christ nourisheth us unto eternal life, both by the grace of the Holy Spirit and by the partaking of his Flesh.

III. 4TH CENT. ST. EPHRAEM. *(On Ezek. x. 2.)*

Those coals of fire, and the man clothed in white linen taking them and pouring them out upon the people, were a figure of the priests of God, through whom the coals of the living and life-giving Body of

the Lord are dispensed. And again, when another
Angel stretches forth his hand, takes the coals of
fire and gives them to the man clothed in white
linen, it implies the mystery that it is not by the
priest himself that the Body can be made from
bread, but by another. That other is the Holy Ghost.

IV. 5TH CENT. ST. CHRYSOSTOM. *(Homily xxiv.*
on 1 Cor. x.)

What is the bread? The Body of Christ? What
do they become who receive it in Communion? The
Body of Christ. Not many bodies, but one body.

V. 6TH CENT. ST. FULGENTIUS. *(Bk. ii. to Moni-*
mus. Ch. xi.)

The spiritual edifying of the Body of Christ in
love is most opportunely prayed for when Christ's
Body, the Church, makes offering of Christ's very
Body and Blood. For the cup which we drink is the
communion of the Blood of Christ; and the
Bread which we break is the communion of
the Body of the Lord. In those to whom
he hath given power to become the sons of
God, the Holy Ghost works what he wrought in
those of whom it is said: The multitude of them
that believed were of one heart and mind.

VI. 4TH CENT. ST. ASTERIUS. *(On Acts ix. 8.*
" They led him by the hand.")

Paul was led by the hand. Pitiable sight—nay,
rather joyous sight! The wolf is bound; the fierce
is tamed: the persecutor of disciples is led as a
disciple. He who had polluted his hands with the
blood of Stephen is led, to drink the Blood of
another.

VII. 4TH CENT. ST. AMBROSE. *(Letter to his sister Marcellina [on translating martyrs' relics].)*

If there be princes of the people, the holy martyrs are they. Noble relics are dug up from an ignoble tomb. The triumphal victims take their place where Christ the Victim lies. But he is on the altar, as he died for all : they are beneath the altar, as redeemed by his Passion.

TRINITY SUNDAY.

I. 6TH CENT. ST. FULGENTIUS. *(Bk. ii. to Monimus. Ch. v.)*

The Catholic faithful ought to know that our bounden duty of the saving Sacrifice is offered by the Catholic Church to the Father, the Son and the Holy Ghost, alike : that is, to the Blessed Trinity. Let us, then, while we offer to the Trinity, who is the One true God, the one sacrifice, refuse to be disturbed by the vain objections of heretics.

II. 4TH CENT. ST. PAULINUS OF NOLA. *(Epistle v.)*

He giveth food to all flesh. Not the food that perisheth, but that which is made for eternal nourishment. It is the Body of the true Bread which came down from heaven and giveth life-giving food to them that hunger after righteousness. This is the Bread and this is the Fountain, whereof whoso eateth is the more hungry, and whoso drinketh the more thirsty.

III. 6TH CENT. TITUS OF BOSTRIA. *(Commentary on St. Luke xxii.)*

No lamb of the flock sanctifieth them that are in Christ, but rather Christ himself offered holily through the mystic Blessing, whereby we are blessed and quickened. For he is made unto us the living Bread, which came down from heaven and giveth life to the world.

IV. 4TH CENT. ST. GAUDENTIUS. *(Tract. ii. to Neophytes. On Exod. xii. 11.)*

The leathern girdle about the loins signifieth the mortification of vices. Therefore we, by God's command, should first mortify the lusts of the flesh, and so receive the Body of Christ.

V. 5TH CENT. RUFFINUS OF AQUILEIA. *(Commentary on Ps. xviii. 11.)*

The Lord hath made darkness his hiding place, in that he hath set in obscurity for us his heavenly Sacrament. Thus it is that we daily handle the Sacrament of the Body and Blood of Christ, yet cannot see with our eyes his light and his glory in which by faith we believe. For we are in the darkness, walking by faith and not by sight.

VI. 5TH CENT. ST. CHRYSOSTOM. *(Homily xxiv. on 1 Cor. x.)*

Here in this place this mystery makes earth heaven for thee. Open then the gates of heaven and look within : thou shalt see what I have said. For that which is of all things in heaven most precious and most to be honoured, that will I show thee set on earth. In a king's palace what is most magnificent is not the walls or the golden roof, but the body of the king sitting on his throne. So in heaven the Body of the King is most magnificent. And it is this thou mayest now behold on earth. For not Angels nor Archangels, nor heavens nor the heaven of heavens do I show thee, but the Lord of all these himself. Seest thou how thou lookest on earth on him who is of more worth than all else? And not only lookest on him, but touchest him; and not only touchest but also eatest him, and having received him returnest home.

VII. 6TH CENT. ST. JOHN CLIMACUS. *(Ladder of Paradise. Step xxviii.)*

How shall he not be changed who with pure hands handles the Body of God?

TRINITY I.

I. 5TH CENT. ST. CYRIL OF ALEXANDRIA. *(Commentary on St. John vi.)*

He that eateth my Flesh and drinketh my Blood abideth in me and I in him. For in like manner as if one should join wax to wax, he would see each to be in the other. Even so, he that receiveth the Flesh of our Saviour and drinketh his precious Blood, will be found one with him, being commingled in some wise and joined to him through that partaking so that he be found in Christ, and Christ, in turn, be found in him.

II. 3RD CENT. ST. CLEMENT OF ALEXANDRIA. *(Schoolmaster. Bk. i. Ch. vi.)*

The Word is to the little one all things, Father and Mother and Schoolmaster and Nurse. Eat, he saith, my Flesh, and drink my Blood. This meet and fitting nourishment the Lord supplieth us, he gives his Flesh, he pours his Blood, and to the little ones of his family naught is lacking for their growth. O wondrous mystery! He bids us lay aside the carnal corruption of the old man, our ancient nourishment, and being made partakers of another and new diet of Christ, receiving him, if it may be, to lay him up within ourselves, to hold within our breast our Saviour.

III. 6TH CENT. ST. AVITUS OF VIENNA. *(Sermon on the Birthday of the Cup.)*

We perceive that he diminished for us naught of the fulness of his substance; all that he took for us, he left to us. Others leave to their heirs their possessions; he left himself, the Flesh and Blood of his Body.

IV. 5TH CENT. ST. CHRYSOSTOM. *(Homily iv. on St. Matt.)*

If he who nourishes worms in his inward parts shall be unable to breathe, how shall we, with the serpent of anger gnawing all our vitals, be able to do any noble thing? How can we be delivered from this pest? By drinking that Draught which is able to destroy worms and serpents within. What Draught, you ask, is this which hath such power? The precious Blood of Christ, if it be taken with the assurance of faith.

V. 4TH CENT. ST. AMBROSE. *(Bk. iv. on the Sacraments. Ch. v.)*

The Lord Jesus himself testifieth to us, that we receive his Body and his Blood. Should we ever have a doubt of his faith and witness?

VI. 5TH CENT. ST. AUGUSTINE. *(Sermon cxxxii. on St. John vi.)*

My Flesh is meat indeed and my Blood is drink indeed. Christ feedeth us daily. His table is that set in the midst of this temple.

VII. 5TH CENT. THEODORET. *(Commentary on Ps. xxiii.)*

The Lord is my shepherd; I shall lack nothing. Christ calleth himself the Shepherd: I am the good Shepherd. And, therefore, all here who receive this saving Food exclaim: The Lord is my Shepherd, I shall lack nothing. All manner of good things are bestowed by this Shepherd on those who are fed by him. He nourishes us with his words; and, more, he giveth us the mystic Food.

TRINITY II.

I. 3RD CENT. ST. CYPRIAN. *(Sermon on the Lord's Supper.)*

We eat on earth the Bread of Angels in the sacrament on earth : in heaven we shall eat the same Bread openly, without a sacrament. When our priesthood has run its course, then shall be abiding sure for ever the presence of our great High Priest, filling and renewing us with his abundance, showing himself openly without any outward coverings, in the sight of all.

II. 4TH CENT. JAMES OF EDESSA. *(Ch. xxi. on Genesis.)*

Melchizedek marvellously showed a type of the bloodless sacrifice of the Body and Blood of Christ. I have always thought that here we have a wonderful and singular symbol of Christ, in that we do not read of Melchizedek receiving either his kingship or his priesthood from any other, or passing it on to any other; whereby he perfectly and absolutely set forth the kingship and priesthood of Christ, which had never beginning nor shall ever end, seeing Christ is a Priest for ever.

III. 5TH CENT. ST. AUGUSTINE. *(Sermon cxxxi. on St. John vi.)*

Of his Body and his Blood the Lord hath given us healing refreshment. To eat this is to be renewed. But in such wise art thou renewed that that which reneweth thee faileth not nor is diminished. Eat the Life, drink the Life : thou hast the Life, and the

Life is undiminished. They said : This is an hard
saying, who can hear it. Hard? Yes, to the hard
of heart : incredible? yes, to the unbelieving.

IV. 5TH CENT. ST. CHRYSOSTOM. *(Homily lxxxii.*
on St. Matthew.)

What shepherd is there who nourishes his sheep
with his own body? Shepherd, do I say? Why
mothers often give their children to others to feed
after birth. Not thus our Lord; he nourishes us
with his own Blood and by all possible ways unites
us to himself. By this mystery he joins to himself
each one of the faithful, and himself nourishes those
whom he has begotten.

V. 4TH CENT. ST. ASTERIUS. *(Sermon on the*
Two Sons.)

The portion of substance which the younger son
asketh of his father is baptism, and the receiving of
the spotless Body.

VI. 4TH CENT. ST. AMBROSE. *(Bk. vii. on*
St. Luke xv.)

The fatted calf is slain that man restored may
by the fellowship of the mysteries feast by the
grace of the Sacrament on the Lord's Flesh rich in
spiritual virtue.

VII. 5TH CENT. ST. AUGUSTINE. *(Bk. ii. Questions*
on the Gospel.)

That fatted calf is both offered to the Father and
feedeth the whole household, in the Lord's Body and
Blood.

TRINITY III.

I. 5TH CENT. ST. CHRYSOSTOM. *(Homily on the Prodigal Son.)*

Bring forth the fatted calf. Slay him that is eaten by them that know him and is never consumed : who maketh blessed them that eat him. They began to feast. Ye who have tasted them know our spiritual dainties, and call to mind the awful mysteries.

II. 4TH CENT. EUSEBIUS OF EMISSA. *(Homily on Gospel for Saturday after 2nd Sunday in Lent.)*

The fatted calf is Christ, full of all virtue and grace. Although he died for us once and now dieth no more, yet is he slain and eaten by the faithful, as oft as he is offered in this Sacrament of the altar. This calf we feed on with body and soul.

III. 5TH CENT. ST. CHRYSOLOGUS. *(Sermon v. on the Prodigal Son.)*

The calf is slain at the father's bidding. For Christ, the Son of God, could not be killed without his Father's will. Hear the Apostle : God spared not his own Son, but freely gave him for us all. This is the calf which is daily sacrificed for our banquet.

IV. 8TH CENT. VEN. BEDE. *(Commentary on St. Luke xv.)*

Be it noted that the clean robe, the ring and the shoes are first put on, and only then is the calf slain.

For unless a man have put on the hope of original immortality, unless he have first sanctified his works with the ring of faith, unless he have proclaimed his faith by confession of it, he cannot have part in the heavenly sacraments.

V. 4TH CENT. ST. AMBROSE. *(Bk. i. On Cain and Abel. Ch. v.)*

Wouldest thou eat? Wouldest thou drink? Come to the Feast of Wisdom, who calleth all, saying: Come, eat of my bread, and drink the wine which I have mingled for you. Be not afraid that in the Banquet of the Church either pleasant foods or noble fellow-guests be wanting. What is nobler than Christ, who in the Banquet of the Church both ministers and is ministered? There shalt thou eat the Bread that strengtheneth man's heart.

VI. 4TH CENT. ST. GAUDENTIUS. *(Sermon ii. to Neophytes.)*

This is that viaticum for our journey, whereby on this road of life we are fed and nourished, until we come to the Lord, departing from this world.

VII. 5TH CENT. ST. CHRYSOSTOM. *(Sermon to the Newly Baptised.)*

Ye take Christ from the altar. Look not alone on what the eye can see. Think not it is mere bread. It is a little thing ye see : great things are given.

TRINITY IV.

I. 4TH CENT. ST. AMBROSE. *(Bk. iv. on the Sacraments. Ch. v.)*

Not in vain sayest thou AMEN; thereby confessing in the spirit that thou receivest the Body of Christ. The priest saith to thee: the Body of Christ; and thou sayest, Amen, that is, It is true. What the tongue confesses, let the heart hold.

II. 5TH CENT. ST. AUGUSTINE. *(Sermon to Children on the Sacrament.)*

Your mystery is set upon the Table of the Lord: ye receive the mystery of the Lord. To that which it is ye reply Amen, and by the reply agree thereto. Thou hearest the words, The Body of Christ; and thou repliest, Amen.

III. 5TH CENT. ST. AUGUSTINE. *(On St. John ii. 24.)*

Catechumens already believe in the name of Christ, but Jesus doth not commit himself unto them. If we should say to a Catechumen, Believest thou in Christ? he answers, I believe. Let us ask him, Dost thou eat the Flesh of the Son of Man and drink the Blood of the Son of Man? He does not understand what we say, for Jesus hath not committed himself to him.

IV. 5TH CENT. ST. AUGUSTINE. *(On Ps. xxii.)*

All the rich of the earth have eaten and worshipped. By the rich of the earth we must understand the proud, if we were right in taking the poor in the verse before to be the humble, of whom it saith in the Gospel, Blessed are the poor in spirit. For then the distinction is apt, when it was said above of the poor, The poor shall eat and be satisfied, and here, All the rich of the earth have eaten and worshipped. The rich indeed are led to the table of Christ, and receive of his Body and Blood. But they worship only, they are not satisfied, since they do not imitate him : for, eating the Poor Man, they disdain to be poor.

V. 7TH CENT. ST. ISIDORE OF SPAIN. *(Letter to the Archdeacon Redemptus.)*

The Lord at supper gave to the disciples his Body under the form of bread and wine, and gave to them power to consecrate it.

VI. 5TH CENT. ST. CHRYSOSTOM. *(Homily xx. to the People of Antioch.)*

Loudly I exclaim, Let no one who hath an enemy approach the holy Table and receive the Body of Christ : let no one who comes have an enemy. Hast thou an enemy? draw not near. Thou desirest to draw near? Be reconciled, and then touch the holy thing. Hear what the Lord saith, If thou bring thy gift to the altar, etc.

VII. 5TH CENT. ST. CYRIL OF ALEXANDRIA. *(Exposition of St. John's Gospel. Ch. vii.)*

We may be partakers of the true Lamb that taketh away the sin of the world only if we have first purged ourselves of the reproach of Egypt, that is, of sin in the soul.

TRINITY V.

I. 3RD CENT. ORIGEN. *(Homily x. on Genesis.)*

Tell me, ye who come to Church only on feast days, are not the other days also feasts? It is the Jewish way, to observe a few fixed days as solemn feasts. Christians feed on the Flesh of the Lamb every day.

II. 5TH CENT. ST. LEO THE GREAT. *(Sermon iii. on the Lord's Passion.)*

More guilty than all, O Judas, thou hast also been more unhappy, since repentance drew thee not back to the Lord, but despair drove thee to the halter. Why dost thou distrust the goodness of him who repelled thee not from communion of his Body and Blood, denied thee not the kiss of peace?

III. 5TH CENT. ST. AUGUSTINE. *(City of God. Bk. xvii. Ch. xx.)*

It saith in Ecclesiastes, It is good and comely for one to eat and to drink. We may well believe that this refers to partaking at that Table which the Mediator of the New Testament setteth forth, of his Body and Blood.

IV. 4TH CENT. ST. BASIL THE GREAT. *(Letter cclxxxix.)*

Good and faithful is it to communicate every day and to receive the holy Body and Blood of Christ.

V.   6TH CENT.   VENANTIUS FORTUNATUS.   *(Bk. x.*
     Ch. i. on the Lord's Prayer.)

Our request for daily bread seems to imply that
we should in all reverence receive communion of his
Body, if possible, every day.   After all, he is our
life, and if we are slow to come to the Eucharist we
make ourselves strangers to our true nourishment.

VI.   5TH CENT.   ST. CHRYSOSTOM.   *(Homily lxxxii.*
      on St. Matthew.)

How many there are who say, I would like to see
Christ's figure, his very form, his garb.   Behold
thou dost see him, thou touchest him, thou eatest
him.   Thou desirest to see his garments : yet he
giveth thee himself, to be touched, to be eaten, to be
received within thee.   Let no one, therefore, draw
near reluctantly or half-heartedly, but all with ardour,
with fervour, with keenness.   For if the Jews, stand-
ing on their feet, with their shoes on and staff in
hand, ate in haste the Passover, much more shouldest
thou be watchful.   They were about to go to Pales-
tine : thou art setting forth for heaven.

VII.   4TH CENT.   ST. EPHRAEM.   *(Sermon iii. on*
       the Lord's Birthday.)

The bread which the Only-Begotten broke in the
desert was consumed and passed away, plentiful as
it was.   Again he brake another Bread which no
age, no lapse of time, shall do away.   The seven
loaves broken in the desert failed.   The One Bread
broken was more than enough for the world : the
more widely it is given, the more plentiful it becomes. One is the Bread he brake and it shall endure
for ever : one the chalice he mingled, and it shall
never be drained.

TRINITY VI.

I. 6TH CENT. ST. FULGENTIUS. *(Sermon on Confessors.)*

Christ giveth himself as Food, that we faint not by the way. He keepeth himself as reward, that we may rejoice in the heavenly home. Christ is our Food : Christ shall be our reward. The Food and Consolation of wayfarers that run their race, he will be the satisfaction and exultation of the Blessed at rest.

II. 3RD CENT. ST. DIONYSIUS OF ALEXANDRIA. *(Letter to Paul of Samosata.)*

God dwelleth in us according to the covenant he made with us, saying, Take and divide. This is the self-emptying of God, being set at our service that we should be able to receive him.

III. 7TH CENT. ST. ELIGIUS. *(Homily viii. on the Lord's Supper.)*

Christ saith, My Flesh is meat indeed, and my Blood is drink indeed; he that eateth my Flesh and drinketh my Blood abideth in me and I in him. Concerning the truth of his Flesh and Blood there is no room left for doubt; for now by the Lord's own declaration and by our faith it is true Flesh, true Blood; and we, receiving these, are made to be in Christ, and Christ in us.

IV. 5TH CENT. ST. AUGUSTINE. *(Sermon cxiii. on the Words of the Gospel.)*

To you the faithful I speak, to you to whom we give the Body of Christ; and I say, Have a fear, mend your ways.

V. 4TH CENT. ST. EPHRAEM. *(On Joel ii. 24.)*

Their barns shall be full of wheat, and their vats shall overflow with wine and oil. This passage hath a sacred meaning, that thou mayest understand that whatever good things are promised to the Jews, Christ hath bestowed them upon his Church : Corn, and wine and mystic oil. Corn, that is the mystery of his most holy Body, his sanctifying Blood in wine, oil also as the most sweet unguent, wherewith in Baptism the initiated are now sealed.

VI. 5TH CENT. ST. JEROME. *(Bk. iii. Dialogue against the Pelagians.)*

The Apostles pray for daily bread, that they may be worthy for receiving the Body of Christ.

VII. 7TH CENT. ST. ISIDORE OF SPAIN. *(On Ecclesiastical Offices.)*

Some say that unless any sin stand in the light the Eucharist should be daily received. They are right, if they receive with religious devotion, in humility, not trusting in their own righteousness in the presumption of pride. But if there are sins such as separate a man from the altar as dead, then penance must be first done, and only after that should this saving medicine be taken.

TRINITY VII.

I. 7TH CENT. ST. GREGORY THE GREAT. *(On Cant. vi. 9. The daughters saw her and blessed her.)*

Holy Church is nourished by the grace that gave her birth, while she is taught by faith, fed with the Flesh of her Spouse, washed in his Blood, instructed in the divine Scripture. Strengthened by this nourishment, she draws out devils, crushes vice, tames the flesh, strengthens the spirit, looks forward to life eternal. And whosoever seeth all this, rightly doth he rise up in admiration and proclaim her blessed.

II. 5TH CENT. ST. CHRYSOSTOM. *(Homily l. on St. Matthew.)*

Let us also touch the hem of the Lord's garment. Nay, if we will, we have him in his entirety. For his Body is now set before us : not his garment only, but his Body; not for us to touch only, but that we may eat and be satisfied. Let us then draw near in faith, each and all who are sick. For if they who touched the hem of his garment drew to themselves such virtue, how much rather they who hold him entire?

III. 5TH CENT. ST. CHRYSOLOGUS OF RAVENNA. *(Sermon xxxiii.)*

The woman touched the Lord's garment and was healed. Unhappy we, who daily handle and take the Body of the Lord, and yet are not healed of our wounds. Not Christ, but faith, is wanting to our weak souls. For he who healed in passing by the woman that laid in wait for him, is much more able to heal the wounded when he abides in us.

IV. 5TH CENT. ST. AUGUSTINE. *(On Ps. xl.)*

Where are the sacrifices of the Jews? They are
gone, for certain : they have certainly been taken
away. And they know it not. They have remained
in the dark. They cannot endure the sun of glory.
Now we are in the light : we have Christ's Body,
we have Christ's Blood.

V. 7TH CENT. ST. ELIGIUS. *(Homily xiv. on the*
Lord's Supper.)

The bitter herbs signify that when we come to
take the Body of Christ, the true Lamb, albeit we
rejoice for our redemption, yet should we have
bitterness in the remembrance of our sins : that
where is the bitterness of penitence there may be
the sweetness of pardon.

VI. 2ND CENT. ST. IGNATIUS. *(Letter to the*
Romans.)

Not in corruptible food, nor in this life's delights
do I take my pleasure. The Bread of God I desire,
the heavenly Bread, which is the Flesh of Jesus
Christ the Son of God, of the stock of David. And
a draught do I desire, his Blood, who is Love incorruptible and Life Eternal.

VII. 3RD CENT. ST. CYPRIAN. *(Epistle liv. to*
Cornelius.)

Those whom we urge and exhort to fight, let us
not leave them unarmed, but fortify them with the
protection of the Body and Blood of Christ. The
Eucharist is meant to be a guard to those who receive it. If we wish to make them safe against the
adversary, let us arm them with the fulness of the
Lord.

TRINITY VIII.

I. 4TH CENT. ST. AMBROSE. *(Sermon viii. on Ps. cxix.)*

Do thou prevent the tempter and his snares : instal first the heavenly Banquet. Attend prepared to receive that which will fortify thee, to eat the Body of the Lord Jesus, in whom is the claim for reconciliation with God and everlasting protection. Receive, ere the tempter come, the Lord Jesus to the hospitality of thy soul : where his Body is, there he is. When the adversary seeth thine abode occupied with the glory of his heavenly presence, he will flee.

II. 6TH CENT. ST. ANASTASIUS OF SINAI. *(Bk. xi. Contemplations.)*

Seest thou not the unconquered and unbroken weapons whereby the Church bruises the serpent's head? The cross, the Body and Blood of Jesus, vows, prayers, vigils and all else she contrives against the serpent.

III. 3RD CENT. ORIGEN. *(Homily xxxviii. on St. Luke.)*

Scripture marvels that the Queen of Sheba came from the ends of the earth to hear the wisdom of Solomon. And when she had seen the meat of his table, his furniture and the ministry of his house, she was astonished and no spirit was left in her.

If we do not gladly embrace the great riches of our Lord, the wondrous furniture of his word, the abundance of his teachings, if we do not eat the

Bread of Life, do not feed on Christ's Flesh and drink his Blood, we ought to know that God is a God of judgment as well as a God of lovingkindness.

IV. 4TH CENT. ST. JAMES OF NISIBIS. *(Sermon xiv. on Easter.)*

Our Lord, when his Body had been eaten and his Blood drunk, was reckoned with the dead. For show us, thou that art skilled and wise in sacred scripture, where are the three days and three nights for which our Lord was among the dead? Between his death and resurrection one whole day and night alone intervened. Yet it cannot be disputed that our Saviour said, As Jonah was three days and three nights in the whale's belly, so shall the Son of Man be in the heart of the earth. However, if the time be reckoned from that hour in which he gave his Body to be eaten and his Blood to be drunk, there are three days and three nights.

V. 5TH CENT. ST. CHRYSOSTOM. *(Homily xlvi. on St. John.)*

I have chosen to be your Brother : for your sakes I took flesh and blood like yours. And again I give you my Flesh and Blood, by which I am become your Kinsman.

VI. 6TH CENT. ST. REMIGIUS OF RHEIMS. *(On 1 Cor. xi.)*

And we, as oft as we draw near to consecrate or receive the Sacrament of the Eternal Gift, which our most tender Lord hath left us to hold in remembrance of him, should approach with all fear and compunction of heart, with all reverence, calling to mind his great love wherewith he hath loved us and offered himself for our redemption.

VII. 4TH CENT. ST. JAMES OF SARAGOSSA. *(Sermon lxvi. on the Lord's Passion.)*

Faith stoops not to questionings. She knows how to believe. She has not learned to investigate. The Apostles, knowing surely that the Son of God spoke the truth, were too wise to make rash and impudent inquiries and investigations. The bread which he brake and said was his Body they recognised as his Body and believed it so to be.

TRINITY IX.

I. 6TH CENT. ST. REMIGIUS OF RHEIMS. *(On 1 Cor. xi.)*

The question is not unreasonably asked, why it was after supper that our Saviour gave the Sacraments of his Body and Blood to the Apostles, or whence has arisen that custom of the universal Church that men are taught to receive these Sacraments fasting, when the Apostles received them after supper. The answer is that the Apostles then communicated after supper, because that typical passover had to be fulfilled before passing on to the Sacraments of the true Passover.

II. 5TH CENT. THEODORET. *(On Ps. xxiii.)*

Thou hast prepared a table before me, and my cup shall be full. This is clear to those who have been initiated into the mysteries, and needs no explanation. They know the mystic food which Christ our Shepherd puts before us.

III. 4TH CENT. ST. AMBROSE. *(On St. Luke ix. The multiplication of the loaves.)*

There is a mystic meaning both in the fact that the people eating are filled, and in the ministry of the Apostles. In their fulness is a sign of the banishing of hunger, for he that receiveth the food of Christ shall not hunger : in the ministry of the Apostles the future distribution of the Lord's Body and Blood is indicated.

IV. 5TH CENT. ST. CHRYSOLOGUS. *(Sermon lxvii. on the Lord's Prayer.)*

He said, I am the Bread which came down from heaven. He is the Bread which, brought to our altars, daily supplieth heavenly food to the faithful.

V. 6TH CENT. PRIMASIUS OF AFRICA. *(Commentary on Rev. viii. 5.)*

The angel took the censer and filled it with fire of the altar. Here the Church hath received all power in heaven and earth while she transacts the Sacrifice of God, the Lord offering himself in the first place.

VI. 5TH CENT. ST. CHRYSOSTOM. *(Catech. ii. to candidates for Baptism.)*

Consider what thou takest in thine hand, and keep that hand free from all grasping avarice. Consider that thou not only takest it in thy hand, but puttest it to thy mouth; and keep thy tongue pure from abusive and evil words.

VII. 5TH CENT. ST. CYRIL OF ALEXANDRIA. *(Commentary on St. John vi.)*

It is written (Prov. x. 3), The Lord will not afflict with hunger the soul of the righteous. For he will set himself before him, as the Bread from heaven, and will nourish the souls of them that fear him.

TRINITY X.

I. 4TH CENT. ST. AMBROSE. *(The Mysteries. Ch. viii.)*

A marvellous thing in truth, that God rained manna for our fathers. Yet they who ate that bread died all in the wilderness. But the Bread which thou receivest, that living Bread which came down from heaven, supplieth the substance of life eternal : it is the Body of Christ.

II. 5TH CENT. ST. LEO THE GREAT. *(Epistle xxiii. to the Clergy of Constantinople.)*

In God's Church such agreement is there in the utterances of all, that the very tongues of infants bear their witness to the truth of the Body and Blood of Christ among the Sacraments of our common faith.

III. 4TH CENT. ST. AMBROSE. *(The Mysteries. Ch. viii.)*

The food which thou receivest is the Body of Christ. Consider now which is the more excellent, the bread of Angels, or the Body of Christ. That manna was from heaven : this is above the heavens. That was of heaven, this of the Lord of heaven. That was in shadow, this in truth. If that which rouses thy marvelling was a shadow, what is this, of which it was a shadow ? The light is more than the shadow, the truth than the figure, the Body of the Maker of heaven more than manna from heaven.

IV. 6TH CENT. PRIMASIUS OF AFRICA. *(Commentary on Rev. ii.)*

Moses and they that were with him did eat the same spiritual food (as the Apostle teacheth us). The visible manna did not hinder them, since they used spiritually a food corporeal. Nor will the spiritual manna of the Lord's Body profit the men of to-day, if they receive it unworthily.

V. 5TH CENT. ST. AUGUSTINE. *(Tract. xxvi. on St. John.)*

Delight thou in the Lord. There is a certain pleasure in the heart which findeth that heavenly Bread sweet. Given one that longeth, that hungereth, that wandering in the desert of life is thirsting, given such a one, he knoweth what I say. If I speak to one who is cold, he knoweth not what I say.

VI. 4TH CENT. ST. EPIPHANIUS OF SALAMIS. *(On Christ's holy Resurrection.)*

We pray you all of your charity to remember earnestly and often our brethren in trouble; and most of all at that dread moment when ye receive at our hands the pearl above all price of Christ's Body.

VII. 5TH CENT. ST. CYRIL OF ALEXANDRIA. *(Bk. iv. Commentary on St. John v.)*

Be devout in resolution, strict and honourable in thy conduct, and so become a partaker of the Blessing, believing that by its power it can not only drive away death, but also diseases. For Christ being in us appeaseth the raging law of the flesh, raiseth devotion to God, bindeth that which is broken, lifteth up that which is fallen.

TRINITY XI.

I. 5TH CENT. ST. CHRYSOSTOM. *(Homily lxxxii. on St. Matthew.)*

Of what purity should he be who hath the enjoyment of this sacrifice? Purer than sunlight should be the hands that distribute this Flesh, the mouth that is filled with this spiritual fire, the tongue stained with this awful Blood.

II. 6TH CENT. ST. ANASTASIUS OF SINAI. *(Sermon on the Sacred Synaxis.)*

Pray for mercy, pray for pardon; pray for remission of sins past and deliverance from sins to come, that thou mayest worthily approach the Sacraments; that with a pure conscience thou mayest take the Body and Blood; that it be to thee for cleansing and expiation, not for judgment. Hear Paul the admirable saying: Let a man examine himself, etc.

III. 7TH CENT. ST. ANDREW OF CRETE. *(For Wednesday in Holy Week.)*

Christ feeds the world with a banquet; he is the heavenly and divine Bread. Ye who love Christ, be there. With pure hearts, with believing mind, let us receive him.

IV. 4TH CENT. ST. EPHRAEM. *(On the holy and life-giving mysteries.)*

Deem not that the bread and the wine thou seest here remain the same: nay, brother, believe it not. By the prayers of the priest, and the coming of the Holy Spirit, bread becomes the Body, wine the Blood.

V. 4TH CENT. EUSEBIUS OF EMISSA. *(Homily v. on Easter.)*

The perpetual Oblation of redemption, the truly singular and perfect Sacrifice, must be weighed by faith, not by sight, be estimated not by outward sight but by inward contemplation. Wherefore rightly doth heavenly authority establish it. My Flesh is meat indeed, and my Blood is drink indeed. Let all unbelieving doubt then depart, since he who is the Author of the gift is himself also the witness of its truth.

VI. 4TH CENT. ST. EPHRAEM. *(Explanation of Deut. xxviii. 3.)*

Blessed shalt thou be in the city, that is, in the Church of Christ. Blessed the flocks of thy sheep; the companies of them that believe in Christ. Blessed thy store; the holy Table and the Body of Christ set thereon.

VII. 5TH CENT. ST. AUGUSTINE. *(Tract. xlv. on St. John.)*

Times have changed, not the faith. The same faith unites both those who believed that Christ should come and those who believe that he has come. That thou mayest know the faith is one, hear the Apostle saying: Our fathers did all drink the same spiritual drink. For they drank of that spiritual rock that followed them: and that rock was Christ. There the rock was Christ: for us it is Christ who is set on the Altar of. God. And they for a great sacrament of the same Christ drank water flowing from the rock: what it is we drink, the faithful know.

TRINITY XII.

I. 4TH CENT. ST. EPHRAEM. *(Bk. i. on Beatitude. Ch. xvii.)*

Blessed is he who with fear and awe and reverence approaches the spotless mysteries of the Saviour; knowing for certain that in him he receiveth life everlasting.

II. 4TH CENT. ST. ATHANASIUS. *(On Maundy Thursday.)*

To-day is the Supper made ready and a table is laid for the whole world. To-day the treasure of the mysteries is disclosed. To-day the Bread of blessedness is set before the Apostles for food. To-day begins the receiving of our spiritual dainties. To-day is uttered that Take, eat, this is my Body; I anticipate the Cross, I distribute my Flesh, I overtake thy selling of me, O Judas, by the pouring forth of my Blood; what thou art about to sell, that, anticipating thee, I freely give.

III. 3RD CENT. ORIGEN. *(Commentary on Ps. lxv.)*

Thou hast prepared meat for them. A spiritual meat is understood. He saith that this hath been prepared, since before the foundation of the world was fore-ordained the mystery of Christ, who is the living Bread coming down from heaven and giving life to the world.

IV. 5TH CENT. ST. CHRYSOLOGUS. *(Sermon lxx. on the Lord's Prayer.)*

After praying for a heavenly kingdom, it is not earthly bread we are bidden to pray for. The Lord forbids that when he says, Take no thought for your life, what ye shall eat. But because he is himself the Bread which came down from heaven, we pray and beseech that we may receive to the health of body and mind that Bread which we are to feed upon daily, that is, in eternity, to-day, that is, in the present life, from the feast of the holy altar.

V. 5TH CENT. ST. AUGUSTINE. *(Sermon lvii. on St. Matthew.)*

Give us this day our daily bread. The prayer for daily bread is to be understood in two senses; for our need of carnal food, or for our need of spiritual nourishment. The faithful know the spiritual nourishment; and you, who are going to receive from the altar of God, will know.

VI. 5TH CENT. ST. CHRYSOSTOM. *(Homily iii. on Ephesians.)*

When the sacrifice is being offered, and Christ becometh our Sacrifice, when thou seest the curtains drawn at the doors (of the iconostasis) consider that high heaven is drawn down, and the Angels descend.

VII. 3RD CENT. ORIGEN. *(Tract. xxxv. on St. Matthew.)*

Judas betrayed Jesus. And like unto him are all they in the Church who plot against their brethren with whom they have often been at the same table of the Body of Christ, shared the same draught of his Blood.

TRINITY XIII.

I. 5TH CENT. VERADATUS *(a Greek Priest).*
    (Letter to the Emperor Leo.)

The Angel taking with the tongs a coal of fire
from the altar (Is. vi. 6) laid it on the prophet's
mouth. Can fingers of flesh approach this coal and
not be burned? It is given to God's holy priests to
hold the sacred Body of the Son of God, nor are
they burned, when they communicate to men the
Food eternal.

II. 4TH CENT. ST. GAUDENTIUS. *(Tract. ii. to
     Neophytes.)*

The Lord saith: Except ye eat my Flesh and
drink my Blood, ye shall not have life. For he
willed that his benefits should endure among us:
he willed that souls should ever be sanctified by the
imaging of his own passion. And, therefore, he
commandeth his disciples, whom he appointed the
first priests of his Church, to celebrate continually
these mysteries of eternal life; and they must be
celebrated by all priests in every one of the Churches
of the whole world, that having daily before our
eyes the Exemplar of Christ's Passion, and bearing
it in our hands, yea, and taking it in the mouth and
the breast, we may hold in indelible remembrance
the work of our redemption.

III. 4TH CENT. EUSEBIUS OF EMISSA *(or anonymous
     author). (Homily v. on Easter.)*

The invisible Priest changeth by his secret power
the visible creatures into the substance of his Body
and Blood, saying, Take, eat, this is my Body, etc.

IV. 5TH CENT. ST. AUGUSTINE. *(Sermon cccxxii.*
on the Birthday of a Martyr.)

To what table of the mighty comest thou? His
who setteth before thee himself. Christ setteth for
thee his table, that is, himself. Come to this table
and be satisfied. Be thou poor and thou shalt be
satisfied. The poor shall eat and be satisfied.

V. 6TH CENT. PRIMASIUS OF AFRICA. *(Com-*
mentary on Heb. x.)

The Divinity of the Word maketh them to be, not
many sacrifices, but one, and that the one Body of
Christ.

VI. 5TH CENT. ST. CYRIL OF ALEXANDRIA. *(Bk. iv.*
Commentary on St. John vi.)

Jesus when he had come to the city of Nain, and
there was carried out that only son of his mother,
touched the bier, saying, Young man, I say unto thee,
Arise. And so not by his word alone does he will
that the dead should be raised, but, to show that his
Body is life-giving, he touches the dead, and sends
life into them, though they be already corrupt,
through himself. But if by the touch alone of his
holy Flesh that which is corrupt is brought to life,
surely with richer benefit shall we receive the life-
giving Blessing, when we even consume it. For he
will utterly transform us who are partakers thereof
into his own good, that is, immortality.

VII. 5TH CENT. ST. AUGUSTINE. *(On Ps. xxii.)*

I will pay my vows, etc. By the vows our Saviour
would have us understand the Sacrifice of his Body,
which is the Sacrament of the faithful. Wherefore
after these words he goeth on to say: The poor
shall eat and be satisfied.

TRINITY XIV.

I. 5TH CENT. ST. CHRYSOSTOM. *(Homily lxxxii. on St. Matthew.)*

Consider how great the honour thou hast obtained : what Table thou enjoyest. What the angels tremble to behold and dare not gaze thereon without fear, for the brightness that streameth from it, with that we are fed, with that we are commingled, and made one body and one flesh of Christ.

II. 4TH CENT. ST. GREGORY OF NYSSA. *(On holy Easter.)*

Christ by a hidden manner of sacrifice, which could not be seen by men, offers himself as host for us, and sacrifices a victim, being at once Priest and Lamb of God, that taketh away the sins of the world. When ordained he this? When he gave to his disciples assembled together his Body to be eaten and his Blood to be drunk; then did he openly declare that the sacrifice of the Lamb was now perfected.

III. 7TH CENT. ST. GREGORY THE GREAT. *(Homily xxii. on the Gospels.)*

What the Blood of the Lamb is ye have learned not by hearing of it, but by drinking. And this Blood is set on either doorpost, when we receive it, not only with the mouth of the body, but also with the lips of the heart. When we receive the Body of the Redeemer, let us afflict ourselves with weeping for our sins, insofar that the very bitterness of penitence may cleanse from the stomach of the inner man the humours of a perverse life.

IV. 4TH CENT. ST. EPHRAEM. *(On Is. xxv. 6.*
"A feast of fat things.")

And this very thing our Lord made clear to us,
when he brake his Body and gave his Blood, saying,
Do this in remembrance of me. This certainly is
the heavenly and rich banquet, imparting to us life :
a feast sure and abiding, the common possession of
all peoples.

V. 7TH CENT. ANDREW OF CAESAREA. *(Commentary on Rev. i. 6.)*

Honour and glory and power becometh him who,
consumed with burning charity, by his own death
delivered our race from the bonds of death, and
exalted us into a royal priesthood; whereby in the
place of the victim of beasts we may offer the living
Victim to God our Father.

VI. 5TH CENT. ST. CHRYSOSTOM. *(Epistle to the
Ephesians. Ch. i.)*

Seest thou not the holy vessels, bright and shining.
Cleaner far than these should our souls be. Why?
Because these vessels are like this for our sake. What
they contain they do not share, they do not perceive;
but we both share and perceive.

VII. 5TH CENT. ST. AUGUSTINE. *(Confessions
ix. 13. On his mother Monica.)*

When the day of her dissolution was at hand she
took no thought for sumptuous trappings for her
body. This was not the subject of her instructions
to us. She only expressed the desire that a remembrance should be made of her at thine altar where
she had worshipped without the intermission of a
day, whence she knew was dispensed the holy Victim,
whereby the handwriting that was against us is
blotted out.

TRINITY XV.

I. 6TH CENT. ST. FULGENTIUS. *(Against Fabian. Bk. viii.)*

The gift of God's love received, let us die to sin and live unto God. For the very partaking of the Lord's Body and Blood implies this to us, that we should die to the world and have our life hid with Christ in God.

II. 7TH CENT. ST. GREGORY THE GREAT. *(Dialogues. Bk. ii. Ch. xxxvii.: on St. Benedict.)*

Six days before his death he bade a grave to be opened for him. And when day by day his weakness increased, on the sixth day he had himself carried by his disciples into the oratory, and there fortified his going forth by the receiving of the Lord's Body and Blood.

III. 8TH CENT. CANON OF EGBERT, *Bishop of York.*

Let priests in mercy give to all sick persons before their departure from this life Viaticum and Communion of Christ's Body.

IV. 6TH CENT. ST. REMIGIUS OF RHEIMS. *(On 1 Cor. xi.)*

With fear and trembling should we approach this awful Sacrament; that the mind of a man may know that it ought to pay reverence to him, whose Body he goeth to receive.

V. 8TH CENT. VEN. BEDE. *(Exposition of 1 Cor. x.)*

Except ye eat my Flesh. How tenderly we hear our Lord inviting us. Who is it invites? Whom doth he invite? And what hath he prepared? The Lord inviteth his servants, and he hath prepared for them as Food—himself. Who would dare to eat his Lord? And yet he saith : He that eateth me, even he shall live by me.

VI. 4TH CENT. ST. AMBROSE. *(Bk. iv. on the Sacraments. Ch. v.)*

Manna fell for the Jews from heaven. A great thing this and calling for veneration. But think : which is the greater, manna from heaven, or the Body of Christ? The Body of Christ who is the Maker of heaven, of course. Then again, he who ate the manna died : but he that eateth this Body shall never die.

VII. 5TH CENT. ST. CHRYSOSTOM. *(Homily xxvii. on 1 Cor. x.)*

If thou drawest near for the Eucharist, do naught unworthy of the Eucharist, and despise not the hungry. To all alike Christ gave, saying, Take, eat. He gave his Body equally to all : but thou dost not give even common bread equally.

TRINITY XVI.

I. 5TH CENT. ST. AUGUSTINE. *(Sermon xv. on the Words of the Lord. Ch. ii.)*

A beggar asketh alms of thee : and thou art God's beggar. For all of us when we pray beg from God. At the gate of the great Father of his family we stand, yea, we prostrate ourselves, as suppliants we make our moan, asking to receive somewhat of him : and that somewhat is God. What does the beggar ask of thee? Bread. And what dost thou ask of God, but Christ, who saith, I am the living Bread.

II. 4TH CENT. ST. AMBROSE. *(On the Mysteries. Ch. ix.)*

The very Flesh of Christ it was which was crucified. Therefore is this the Sacrament of his very Flesh. The Lord Jesus himself proclaims, This is my Body.

III. 5TH CENT. ST. AUGUSTINE. *(On Ps. ci.)*

We feed from the cross of the Lord, since we eat his Body.

IV. 5TH CENT. ST. CYRIL OF ALEXANDRIA. *(Letter to Bishop Arsomotus.)*

I hear of some who say that the mystic Blessing profits nothing for sanctification, if any of it be kept to another day. They are mad who make such an assertion. For Christ is not altered, nor does his holy Body suffer change.

V. 5TH CENT. ST. AUGUSTINE. *(On Ps. xxxiv.)*

Let us draw nigh unto him, that we may receive his Body and his Blood. But someone will say: how can I draw nigh to him? I am burdened with so much evil, such great sins, my grievous crimes cry out from my conscience; how dare I draw nigh to God? How? If thou hast humbled thyself by penance. But, you say, I blush to do penance. Draw nigh to him and thou shalt be enlightened, and thy face shall not be ashamed. Draw nigh with faith that presseth forward, with heart that yearneth, with charity that runneth. Taste and see that the Lord is gracious.

VI. 7TH CENT. ST. ISIDORE OF SPAIN. *(On Numbers.)*

That cluster of grapes which hanging on the middle of a branch of wood two carriers bore from the Land of Promise, what doth it signify? That cluster hanging from the wood, as Christ from the wood of the cross, is the Saviour promised to the nations. The two bearers going forward under the weight of that cluster are the two peoples. That in front is the Jewish nation, blind, with its back turned, unknowing of the grace of him that hangs there, yet oppressed by his weight, to answer to his judgment. But the man behind stands for the people of the Gentiles, who believing and having Christ before their eyes at once bear him and see him, and follow their Lord as servants, their Master as disciples. This is the cluster poured out for our salvation which shed by the burden of the cross the wine of his Blood, and gave to the Church the chalice pressed of his Passion.

VII. 5TH CENT. ST. JEROME. *(Bk. ii. Against Jovinian.)*

We all receive in equal degree the Body of Christ, although this one Body be diverse in its fruit according to the merits of those that receive.

H

TRINITY XVII.

I. 4TH CENT. MARK THE HERMIT. *(Book on Melchizedek.)*

As Melchizedek offered bread and wine to those that returned from battle, after conquering the five kings: so Christ to those returning from the spiritual warfare, having overcome the adversary, giveth his holy Bread, saying, Eat ye all of this. Again, as Abraham paid tithes to him that offered bread, so they who imitate the faith and obedience of Abraham and receive from Christ, the true Melchizedek, the Bread of life, which is Christ himself, in the holy Eucharist, offer to him the five outward senses, and the like number of interior senses, as tithes of their nature.

II. 5TH CENT. ST. NILUS. *(Epistle ccxxxiv.)*

It is impossible for the believer to be saved and obtain the heavenly kingdom, unless with fear and desire he partake of the mystic and spotless Body and Blood of Christ our God.

III. 5TH CENT. ST. CHRYSOSTOM. *(On the healing of the man sick of the palsy.)*

Christ not only raised up the man with the palsy, but said first, That ye may know that the Son of Man hath power on earth to forgive sins. Therefore he cured him, mainly to show that he had like authority with the Father. All these things let us diligently keep in memory, and so draw near often to this holy place. For what troubling thoughts so ever vex our soul, when we come to this place, can easily be shaken off, since now too is Christ here, and he who draweth near to him with faith shall obtain easy healing.

IV.   6TH CENT.   ST. CAESARIUS OF ARLES. *(Homily xii. Warning against going out in the middle of Mass.)*

If ye attend with diligence ye will recognise that the Mass takes place not when the sacred lections are read in the Church, but when the gifts are offered, and the Body and Blood of the Lord is consecrated.

V.   5TH CENT.   ST. CHRYSOSTOM.   *(Homily li. on St. Matthew.)*

Let us draw nigh to God and fall down at his feet, not with the body alone, but also in heart and mind. Let us consider whom we approach, and for whom, and with what end in view. We come to God, whom the Seraphim beholding turn away their faces as not enduring his brightness. We come to God, at the sight of whom the earth trembles. We come that we may be delivered from hell, that we may obtain remission of our sins; that we may obtain heaven and the good things there laid up. Let us fall down therefore with body and soul.

VI.   5TH CENT.   ST. AUGUSTINE.   *(Sermon ccclxxii. on the Birth of Christ.)*

The multitude of the Gentiles hath filled the Church. It hath received of the Lord's Table no scanty feast, no mean drink. But it hath tasted the Flesh and Blood of the Shepherd himself, of the very Christ slain.

VII. 7TH CENT. ST. GREGORY THE GREAT. *(Homily
xiv. on the Gospels.)*

The Good Shepherd gave his life for his sheep,
that in our Sacrament he might give his Body and
Blood and satisfy with the nourishment of his Flesh
the sheep whom he had redeemed.

TRINITY XVIII.

I. 4TH CENT. ST. CYRIL OF JERUSALEM. *(Catech. v.)*

The priest exclaims, Lift up your hearts. For truly at this exceeding solemn moment one's heart should be lifted up to God, and not concerned with earth and earthly matters. It is as though the priest bade that all should at that time lay aside the cares of this life and domestic worries, and turn their heart to the merciful God in heaven above. Then ye reply, We lift them up unto the Lord. Then let none be present so minded that while with his lips he says, We lift them up unto the Lord, his mind is filled with the cares of this life.

II. 4TH CENT. EUSEBIUS OF EMISSA. *(Homily on St. Matthew xxii.)*

How camest thou in hither, not having on a wedding garment? This he seems to say especially to those who unworthily approach the Sacrament of Christ's Body and Blood.

III. 5TH CENT. ST. LEO THE GREAT. *(Sermon xii. for Lent.)*

He that is about to enter on the nuptial feast, let him be adorned with the robe of virtues. For although the lovingkindness of the Bridegroom inviteth all to communion of the royal Banquet, yet all who are called must strive that they be not found unworthy of the gift of the holy Food.

IV. 5TH CENT. ST. CHRYSOLOGUS. *(Sermon clxi. on St. Luke xvii. 7—10.)*

The Apostles served the Lord, sitting at meat, all the time that in the midst of heathen fires and altars they made ready the Feast of the Lord on the holy tables of the Church for a perpetual memory. What this Feast is, he that is of the faithful knoweth. If any know not, let him become one of the faithful.

V. 5TH CENT. ST. AUGUSTINE. *(Bk. ii. on Questions of the Gospel.)*

We may take Lazarus to signify the Lord Jesus. The sores are his Passion. The dogs that licked them are the Gentiles, whom the Jews pronounced unclean. Yet, the world over, do they lick, with the sweetness of true devotion, in the Sacrament of his Body and Blood, the Lord's wounds.

VI. 6TH CENT. PRIMASIUS OF AFRICA. *(Commentary on Rev. vii. 15.)*

Therefore are they before the throne of God. The Church is before the throne of God, serving him in this vale of tribulation day and night, that is, in prosperity and adversity. They shall not hunger, for they are fed with living Bread: I am, saith Christ, the living Bread which came down from heaven. Neither shall they thirst, for they are inebriated with his wondrous chalice.

VII. 5TH CENT. ST. AUGUSTINE. *(Tract. xlviii. on the Psalms.)*

The poor shall eat and be satisfied. What do they eat? The faithful know.

TRINITY XIX.

I. 3RD CENT. ORIGEN. *(Homily ii. on Ps. xxxviii.)*

I will confess my wickedness and be sorry for my
sin. If in thy body any spot or sore arise, thou art
anxious and considerest what remedy should be
applied to restore to thy body its original health.
When thy soul is sick, art thou content? Dost thou
despise hell, or hold in contempt and smile at the
torments of eternal fire? Dost thou not fear to
communicate of the Body of Christ, coming to the
Eucharist?

II. 4TH CENT. ST. ATHANASIUS. *(Against the
Arians.)*

We have the first-fruits of the Bread of heaven in
this present life, when we are made partakers of the
Lord's Flesh, as he himself said : The Bread which
I will give is my Flesh.

III. 3RD CENT. ST. CLEMENT OF ALEXANDRIA.
(Schoolmaster. Bk. i. Ch. v.)

Christ calls himself allegorically the vine; for as
the vine gives wine, so the Lord his Blood. And
either cup is for man's good, wine for his body,
Blood for his soul.

IV. 6TH CENT. ST. JUSTUS. *(On Cant. ii. 3.)*

His fruit was sweet to my taste. The Lord saith
in the Gospel, I am the vine, ye are the branches :

111

he that abideth in me and I in him, the same bringeth forth much fruit. Whatsoever fruit the righteous bear in good works, all is to be referred to Christ. In whose fruits a sweetness incomparable is felt. For those saints who have been wont to ponder on that which they have tasted with the mouth, to meditate upon the things of Christ, know a sweetness passing measure from his fruit.

V. 5TH CENT. ST. JEROME. *(Epistle lxii.)*

Without charity we cannot know what it is to be at peace, without being at peace we cannot know communion. If we cannot offer our gifts without being at peace, much less can we receive the Body of Christ.

VI. 4TH CENT. ST. EPHRAEM. *(Bk. i. on Beatitude. Ch. xvi.)*

Blessed is he who keepeth himself pure and undefiled from every stain of sin, that he may with confidence receive into his house the King of glory, our Lord Jesus Christ.

VII. 6TH CENT. ST. CAESARIUS OF ARLES. *(Sermon for a Dedication.)*

That we may receive our Lord's Body and Blood not to judgment but for our healing, let us strive so far as possible, with his help, that he suffer no harm in us from evil deeds. For everyone who doeth evil doeth injury to Christ. And if thou wouldest not suffer injury in thy house, so, too, the Lord would not suffer it in his house, that is, in thy soul.

TRINITY XX.

I. 4TH CENT. ST. AMBROSE. *(Bk. viii. Commentary on St. Luke xvii. 37.)*

Wheresoever the body is, thither will the eagles be gathered together. Let us think first what the eagles are and then define what is the body. The souls of the righteous are compared to eagles, inasmuch as they aim for the heights and leave low things. Will you not see the eagles round the Body when he shall come in the clouds, and every eye shall see him, and they that pierced him? There is the Body also of which it was said : My Flesh is meat indeed, and my Blood is drink indeed. Around this Body are the true eagles, borne up on the wings of the spirit.

II. 5TH CENT. ST. AUGUSTINE. *(Sermon cccxxix. on the Martyrs' Feast Day.)*

Great is the Table where the feast is the Lord of the Table. No one else feeds his guests upon himself. Our Lord does. He is the host inviting us : he is the meat and drink.

III. 5TH CENT. ST. CHRYSOSTOM. *(Homily i. on the Betrayal of Judas.)*

To the pure oblation we come. Let us render our soul holy : even in one day can this be done. How, and on what lines? If thou hast anything against an enemy, take away thine anger, end thine enmity, that thou mayest take healing from the holy Table : for thou drawest nigh to a solemn and holy sacrifice. Take reverent heed to the argument of this oblation. Christ as slain lieth here. For whom and why was

113

he slain? That he might bring peace to heaven and earth : that he might make thee the friend of the angels : that he might reconcile thee to the God of all : that of thee, his enemy and adversary, he might make a friend. He laid down his life for those who hated him : and dost thou keep enmity against thy fellow-servant? How canst thou then approach the Table of peace?

IV. 5TH CENT. ST. CYRIL OF ALEXANDRIA. *(Bk. x. Ch. ii.)*

That which by nature is corruptible can only be quickened if it be bodily united to the Body of him who by nature is the Life.

V. 4TH CENT. ST. AMBROSE. *(Sermon xviii. on the Psalms.)*

Mine is the wondrous sharing in the heavenly sacraments. Mine the honour of a heavenly Table. Christ my food, Christ my drink. The Flesh of God my food, the Blood of God my drink. Daily is Christ given me. My food is that which fattens not the body but strengthens man's heart.

VI. 5TH CENT. ARNOBIUS OF GAUL. *(Commentary on Ps. xxxiv.)*

Taste the Body of the Life, and ye shall see how sweet the Lord is.

VII. 4TH CENT. ST. HILARY. *(Sermon on Ps. cxxviii.)*

It is the Table of the Lord from which we receive the Food of a Living Bread, which hath the virtue, that since it is Living Bread it maketh them who receive it to live.

114

TRINITY XXI.

I. 7TH CENT. ST. ISIDORE OF SPAIN. *(Bk. ii. on Ecclesiastical Offices.)*

The order of Presbyters took its beginning from the sons of Aaron. For those who were called priests in the Old Testament are those who are now called Presbyters. To these, as to the Bishops, the dispensation of the mysteries of God is committed. For they are set over the Church of Christ; and in the consecration of the divine Body and Blood are sharers with the Bishops; as also in the instruction of the nations and in the office of preaching.

II. 4TH CENT. ST. EPHRAEM. *(Homily on the Day of Judgment.)*

Our soul is the bride of the immortal Bridegroom. The nuptials are the heavenly sacraments, for when we eat his Body and drink his Blood, he is in us, and we in him.

III. 4TH CENT. ST. AMBROSE. *(Bk. iii. on Virginity.)*

That woman who suffered from an issue of blood was straightway healed, because she came with faith. And do thou with faith touch his garment. Then shall the flux of worldly pleasures be dried up by the warmth of the saving Word of God, if only with faith thou come, if with a like devotion thou touch only the very hem of his garment: if in holy fear thou fall down at the Lord's feet. Where are the feet of the Lord, save where the Body of Christ is?

IV. 5TH CENT. ST. CHRYSOLOGUS. *(Sermon xxxiv. on the woman with the issue of blood.)*

O how well hath this woman taught us what power there is in the Body of Christ, showing what it was even in his garment. Let Christians, who daily touch the Body of Christ, hear what wondrous healing they can obtain from that Body itself, since this woman obtained healing from Christ's garment alone.

V. 5TH CENT. ST. CHRYSOSTOM. *(Homily xvii. on Heb. x.)*

I want to say a few words to you who are initiated into the mysteries. Many are partakers of this Sacrifice once only in the whole year; others twice; others again often. What then? Which of these do we most approve, those who communicate once a year, or those who communicate twice, those who communicate often, or those who communicate seldom? Neither the one nor the other: but those who communicate with a clean conscience, with a pure heart, with a life free of reproach. Those who are such, let them always come. Those who are not such, not even once a year.

VI. 5TH CENT. ST. LEO THE GREAT. *(Sermon iv. on the Passion.)*

Of all virtues, the most excellent are loving mercy and chaste purity. Let us then equip ourselves with these aids, that by the work of charity and the splendour of purity we may be lifted up as on two wings, and from earthly become heavenly. Anyone filled by the help of God's grace with this desire honours aright the paschal sacrament. The destroying angel enters not his threshold, marked with the

Blood of the Lamb and the seal of the cross. Therefore, with bodies and souls purified, let us embrace
the wondrous sacrament of our salvation.

VII. 6TH CENT. ST. ANASTASIUS OF SINAI.
    (Question vii.)

They who were partakers of the ancient sacrifice
first made expiation and cleansed themselves utterly.
But thou comest to the Victim, whom the very
angels revere, and receivest Christ's Body and
Blood.

TRINITY XXII.

I. 4TH CENT. ST. JAMES OF SARAGOSSA. *(Sermon lxvi. on the Lord's Passion.)*

From that moment when Christ took bread and proclaimed it his Body, it was not bread but his Body, and the Apostles ate it and marvelled the while. They ate his Body who sat with them at the table : they drank his Blood whose voice they heard at the same time instructing them.

II. 3RD CENT. ST. IRENAEUS. *(Bk. v. against Heresies. Ch. ii.)*

That cup, of what he created, he proclaims to be his Blood poured out, and by it he nourishes our blood : that bread, of his creation, he proclaims his Body and nourishes our bodies thereby. When the mingled chalice and the broken bread receives the word of God it becomes the Eucharist of Christ's Body and Blood, whereby the substance of our flesh is nourished and lives; how can they deny that the flesh can receive the gift of Christ, which is eternal life, the flesh nourished by Christ's Body and Blood?

III. 4TH CENT. ST. AMBROSE. *(Bk. iv. on the Sacraments. Ch. iv.)*

He spake the word, and they were made; he commanded, and they were created. Dost thou not understand how mighty is the heavenly word in operation? If the heavenly word operated in other matters, operates it not in the heavenly sacraments? Therefore hast thou been taught that from bread becomes the Body of Christ, and that what was put into the chalice as wine and water becomes by the consecration of the heavenly word his Blood. Thou hast been taught, therefore, that what thou receivest is the Body and Blood of Christ.

IV. 5TH CENT. ST. CHRYSOSTOM. *(Homily lxxxii. on St. Matthew.)*

Therefore let us in everything obey God and not contradict him, even although what he says seem contrary to our reason and intelligence : let his word prevail over our reason and intelligence. For his word cannot deceive, but our perception is easily deceived. Therefore, when he says, This is my Body, let us yield, let us believe.

V. 3RD CENT. MAGNES, *Priest of Jerusalem. (Bk. iii. Apology against Theostatus.)*

This is no figure of his Body and Blood, but truly the Body and Blood of Christ. There is no other creator of the earth than this. There is no creature that was not created by the Son of God.

VI. 3RD CENT. ST. CYPRIAN. *(Epistle lxiii. to the Council.)*

The image of the sacrifice of Christ had gone before (Gen. xiv.) being constituted in bread and wine. And completing and fulfilling it the Lord offered bread and the chalice mingled of wine; and he who is the fulness of truth fulfilled the truth of the prefigured image.

VII. 4TH CENT. ST. GAUDENTIUS. *(Tract. ii. to Neophytes.)*

When Christ gave to his disciples the consecrated bread and wine, he saith : This is my Body, this is my Blood. Let us believe, I beseech you, in him in whom we have believed; the truth knoweth no lie.

TRINITY XXIII.

I. 4TH CENT. ST. AMBROSE. *(Commentary on Ps. xxxix.)*

We have seen the chief of priests coming to us: we have seen and heard him offering for us his Blood. Let us priests follow as best we may; let us offer sacrifice for the people, unworthy though we be, yet honourable by our sacrifice. For although Christ is now visibly offered, yet is he offered on earth, when the Body of Christ is offered. It is clear, too, that he offers in us, as it is his word that sanctifies the sacrifice which is offered.

II. 5TH CENT. ST. AUGUSTINE. *(Bk. xvii. Ch. xx. City of God.)*

A man hath no better thing under the sun than to eat and drink (Eccles. viii. 15). What more worthy of belief than that this refers to the partaking of that Table which our Priest and the Mediator of the New Testament setteth forth according to the order of Melchizedek with his Body and Blood? For the sacrifice hath succeeded to all those sacrifices of the Old Testament, which were offered foreshadowing that which should come. Wherefore we recognise those words of the psalm as spoken in prophecy by our Mediator, Sacrifice and offering thou wouldest not: but a body hast thou prepared me; since in place of all those sacrifices and offerings his Body is offered, and given to communicants.

III. 5TH CENT. ST. CHRYSOSTOM. *(Homily vi. against the Anomaei.)*

Thou art about to receive thy King in communion. And when the King enters the soul, it should be hushed in great tranquillity.

IV. 5TH CENT. ST. CYRIL OF ALEXANDRIA. *(Bk. iii. Commentary on St. John vi.)*

He that cometh to me shall not thirst. What, then, doth Christ promise? Nothing corruptible, but rather that Blessing which is in the partaking of his holy Flesh and Blood, which recalleth the whole man to incorruption.

V. 4TH CENT. ST. EPHRAEM. *(Sermon against Questioners.)*

He who hath the eye of faith plainly and clearly beholdeth the Lord, and in full and undoubting faith eateth the Body of the immaculate Lamb, free from all curious questioning of the divine and holy faith.

VI. 5TH CENT. ST. LEO THE GREAT. *(Sermon vi. on the fast of the seventh month.)*

Ye should so receive at the Holy Table that ye doubt not at all concerning the verity of Christ's Body and Blood. What the faith believeth, the mouth receiveth : and in vain is Amen replied by those who dispute against what is received.

VII. 6TH CENT. ST. FULGENTIUS. *(Bk. viii. against Fabian.)*

The sacrifice then is offered that the Lord's death be shown. While at the time of sacrifice we make commemoration of his death, we pray that charity be given us, earnestly entreating that through that charity which led Christ to die for us, we also may be crucified to the world, and the world to us.

I

TRINITY XXIV.

I. 4TH CENT. ST. EPHRAEM. *(On Is. xi. 7.)*

The lion shall eat straw like the ox, since the righteous and sinners alike feed on the living Body which is on the altar.

II. 4TH CENT. PHILO OF CARPATHIA. *(On Cant. vii.)*

Christ is the Head of the Church: to him are most closely joined all the holy members of the faithful, and those especially who as faithful ministers administer his divine Body and the Blood of eternal salvation: the Food and Drink that bringeth healing to the Christian people, known only to those who have tasted it.

III. 5TH CENT. ST. CHRYSOSTOM. *(Homily xlvi. on St. John.)*

Let us go away from the holy Table like lions breathing fire, terrible to the devil; considering that Christ is our Head, and how great love he hath shown to us.

IV. 5TH CENT. THEODORET. *(On Cant. Bk. i. 1.)*

Let him kiss me with the kisses of his mouth. Thus speaketh the Bride, entreating the Father of the Bridegroom. She hath heard David telling in the psalms of his beauty and strength: Thou art fairer than the children of men, etc. The bride hath learned that this fair and lovely Bridegroom is God and the Son of God before all eyes. When, therefore, she hath learned of his beauty, his wealth, his eternal power, incorruptible and unending, she hungereth to see him and to rush into his embrace and give him spiritual kisses. And if anyone, being earthly-minded, be troubled at the mention of kisses, let him rather consider how at the time of the mysteries we take the Body of the Bridegroom, clasp it and kiss it.

V. 5TH CENT. ST. CHRYSOSTOM. *(Homily l. on St. Matthew.)*

Christ himself is here, commanding you : Call no man your father on earth. Not that parents are to be despised, but that thou shouldest set before them all thy Maker, who enrolled thee among his sons : for he who gave the greatest thing, his very self, will deign to give thee his own Body. Hear we then, both priests and those subject to them, of what gift we are counted worthy. Let us hear and let us be filled with reverential awe : his own holy Flesh hath he given us to eat.

VI. 5TH CENT. ARNOBIUS THE YOUNGER. *(Commentary on Ps. lxxxiii.)*

The sanctuary of God is where the sacraments of the mysteries are laid up. There is the heavenly Flesh : there the Blood divine.

VII. 7TH CENT. ANDREW OF CAESAREA. *(Commentary on Rev. v.)*

To him that overcometh will I give the hidden manna. The hidden manna is the Bread of heavenly life which for our salvation came down from heaven and is most meet to be eaten.

TRINITY XXV.

I. 5TH CENT. THEODORET. *(Commentary on 1 Cor. xi.)*

Let us flee from all things that militate against the faith. And let us have a care for the poor: and first cleansing our consciences let us be partakers of the divine sacraments, that we may worthily receive the good Lord within us.

II. 7TH CENT. ST. ELIGIUS. *(Homily viii. on the Lord's Supper.)*

See, brethren, if ye that are of the faithful keep away from the Lord's Body, it is to be feared lest ye die of hunger; but if ye receive it unworthily, it is to be feared lest ye eat unto condemnation.

III. 5TH CENT. ST. CYRIL OF ALEXANDRIA. *(Bk. x. Ch. ii. On St. John xv.)*

Paul writes that the Gentiles are made of one body and partakers and fellow-heirs with Christ. How are they made of one body with him? By partaking of the Blessing of the mysteries are they made one body with him.

IV. 5TH CENT. ST. AUGUSTINE. *(On the Presence of God.)*

This sacrament is far from the hearts of the proud wise folk, who are not Christian and thereby not truly wise. I speak of those wise folk who have known God, in that knowing God, as the Apostle saith, they glorified him not as God, nor gave thanks to him. Thou knowest in what sacrifice it is said:

Let us give thanks unto our Lord; and from the humility of this sacrifice their strutting self-importance is far removed.

V. 5TH CENT. ST. PROCLUS OF CONSTANTINOPLE.
    (Book on the delivery of the Divine Liturgy.)

The Apostles, before they were scattered over the world, with one accord betook themselves to prayer for a whole day. And since they had found much consolation in that mystic sacrifice of the Lord's Body, they sang the Liturgy with the outpouring of long prayer. For they deemed that this divine transaction should be set before all else.

VI. 5TH CENT. ST. CHRYSOSTOM. *(Homily on the Baptism of Christ.)*

Christ called us eagles, when he said, Wheresoever the body is, thither shall the eagles be gathered together, because we should ascend into heaven, and fly up on high, borne by the wings of the spirit. But we, on the contrary, like serpents, creep on the ground. Dear man, what doest thou? When Christ is present, and the angels stand around, when that awful table is set, and thy brethren make acquaintance with the mysteries, dost thou leave them and go away?

VII. 7TH CENT. ISYCHIUS, *Priest of Jerusalem.*
      (Bk. vi. on Levit.)

In ignorance he receiveth the mystery, who knoweth not its power and dignity; who is ignorant that this is the Body and the Blood according to the truth : he receiveth the mysteries, but knoweth not the virtue of the mysteries. To him Solomon saith, or rather the Holy Spirit in Solomon, When thou sittest to eat with a ruler, consider diligently what is before thee. (Prov. xxiii. 1.)

TRINITY XXVI.

I. 4TH CENT. ST. GAUDENTIUS. *(Tract. ii. to Neophytes.)*

God said in Exodus (xii.), Ye shall eat it in haste. When he saith that it is to be eaten in haste, he commandeth that we should take the sacrament of the Lord's Body and Blood, not with slow heart or languid lips, but with all eagerness of soul, as men who truly hunger and thirst after righteousness.

II. 5TH CENT. ST. CHRYSOSTOM. *(Homily xxix. on Genesis.)*

Noah drank of the fruit of the vine and was drunken. Not that the vine is evil, or wine evil, but the abuse thereof is evil. If it do harm, the reason is man's intemperance. Consider another case where wine was of use, for by it is perfected the material of the good things of our salvation. They who are initiated into the mysteries know what I mean.

III. 5TH CENT. ST. CHRYSOLOGUS. *(Sermon xcv.)*

I am the Bread which came down from heaven, saith Christ. God ever giveth greater things than he is asked for. He promises his disciples : Ye who have followed me to the end shall eat and drink at my table in my kingdom. Christian, he who here hath given thee himself to eat, what that is his can he deny thee hereafter? And he who hath given thee so great a food for thy journeying here, what hath he not prepared for thee in that everlasting rest?

IV. 5TH CENT. ST. AUGUSTINE. *(Tract lxxxiv. on St. John xv.)*

We read in the Proverbs of Solomon, When thou sittest to eat with a ruler (Prov. xxiii. 1), consider diligently what is before thee. What is sitting to eat but coming humbly to the altar? And what is diligently to consider what is set before thee but meetly to ponder on the great grace received thereby?

V. 5TH CENT. ST. CYRIL OF ALEXANDRIA. *(Sermon on the Mystic Banquet.)*

Wisdom hath builded an house. . . She hath prepared her table . . . saying : Come, eat of my bread. These things, beloved, are symbolic of what is now done. Divine gifts are set forth, a table is made ready, a life-giving chalice is mingled, the King of Glory prepareth, the Son of God receiveth, God Incarnate, the Word, inviteth. He who is the Wisdom of God the Father and hath builded himself a temple not made with hands, distributeth his own Body in fashion of bread, and offereth his life-giving Blood as wine.

VI. 3RD CENT. ST. HIPPOLYTUS. *(Commentary on Gen. xlix. 20.)*

These words : His bread shall be fat, and he shall yield royal dainties, I believe mystically imply the sacraments of the New Testament of our Saviour. Fat standeth for good and comely. And what bread is better than ours? For our Bread is the Lord, as he himself saith : I am the Bread of Life. Who else is to give food to royal princes, save our Lord Jesus

Christ? Not only to those who believe of the Gentiles, but also to those of the circumcision, who hold by faith their royal estate.

VII. 4TH CENT. ST. GAUDENTIUS. *(Tract. ii. to Neophytes.)*

He that is consecrated sanctifieth them that consecrate.

LAUS CHRISTO.

INDEX OF AUTHORS AND SOURCES CITED BY BAVERSTOCK

129